BREAKING
THE · RING

BOOKS BY JOHN BARRON

KGB: The Secret Work of Soviet Secret Agents
Murder of a Gentle Land (with Anthony Paul)
MiG Pilot
KGB Today: The Hidden Hand
Breaking the Ring

BREAKING THE · RING

John Barron

Boston / 1987

HOUGHTON MIFFLIN COMPANY

Library of Congress Cataloging-in-Publication Data
Barron, John, date.
Breaking the ring.
Includes index.
1. Walker, John Anthony, 1937–   2. Walker
family.   3. Whitworth, Jerry.   4. Espionage — Soviet
Union — History — 20th century.   5. Espionage — United
States — History — 20th century.   6. United States.
Federal Bureau of Investigation.   7. United States.
Navy — Communication systems.   I. Title.
UB271.R92W342   1987   327.1'2'0924   86-33803
ISBN 0-395-42110-1

Printed in the United States of America

To all who serve silently and valiantly
so that their fellow citizens may
live in freedom and justice

Acknowledgments

Throughout the process culminating in publication of this book, Houghton Mifflin Company has done all that a writer could ask or desire. I am grateful to its superb professionals and especially to my editor, Robie Macauley.

I am also grateful to friends and colleagues at *Reader's Digest*. Managing Editor William Schulz creatively criticized each chapter while constantly offering me counsel and encouragement. Associate Editor G. William Gunn painstakingly documented the manuscript and purged first drafts of numerous errors. Patricia McLamara of the Washington office expertly typed the entire manuscript and kindly assisted me in countless ways.

Finally, I gratefully acknowledge the assistance of all those who gave me guidance and facts in confidence, out of the selfless belief that the public ought to have the truth about the worst known espionage case in American history.

Contents

BREAKING
THE · RING

1

A Letter from RUS

IN SAN FRANCISCO by midsummer 1984 John Peterson and Bill Smits knew. In Washington the few people who had seen the full file probably also understood. But lacking proof, no one dared proclaim the truth.

Eminent and earnest scientists could demonstrate mathematically that American military ciphers, the product of genius and the world's most powerful computers, were impenetrable, unbreakable. Absent evidence, anyone who suggested otherwise would condemn himself to permanent ineffectuality and provide a feast for professional vultures. You could hear them: *Burnout. Gone around the bend. Fine mind but fanaticism did him in; always saw things in black and white. A form of rank McCarthyism. Just shows again how fortunate we are that management holds a tight rein.*

So they kept silent. But they knew. The United States was in mortal peril.

Janet Fournier must be credited with discerning the first clue. Someone less conscientious easily could have ignored it.

From childhood on, Janet Fournier had been conscientious. She grew up in Avalon, Texas, a rural hamlet of some three hundred people, and her high school graduating class consisted of nine students. Her grandfather was a sheriff, her father a constable, then justice of the peace. Her father so looked the part of a leathery Texas lawman that directors collared him for a bit role in the gangster film *Bonnie and Clyde*.

Wanting to be like her father, Janet quit college during her junior year to join the Federal Bureau of Investigation as a typist in Dallas. She matured into a full-bodied young woman distinguished by happy green eyes and red hair. In the office they came to count on her to stay until all work was done; to correct misspellings and ungrammatical sentences on her own initiative; to greet visitors graciously.

Diligence and reliability earned her a promotion to secretary and in 1976 a coveted assignment to the U.S. embassy in Paris. She mastered French, learned about fine wines and cuisine, galleries and museums. She also learned a little about cryptography and cipher machines used by the legal attaché.

At the end of her four-year tour in France, the FBI gave her a choice of cities in the United States, and she chose San Francisco. FBI agents volunteered to help move her into an apartment in August 1980. Later, she married one of them, Special Agent Pierre Fournier.

Elevated from a secretary to an investigative assistant in counterintelligence, Janet administered the Complaint Desk. She had to politely fend off abusive calls from psychotics, listen to the ravings of drunks, sympathize with grieving widows who called only because they craved companionship. Additionally, she had to evaluate and dispose of the many letters, signed and unsigned, emanating from seriously disturbed people. Some fabricated lurid charges of wrongdoing against former spouses, neighbors, or associates. Others reported, often graphically, imaginary details of crimes or conspiracies about which they fantasized.

Virtually all of the anonymous letters, even the coherent ones, safely could be discarded in the "nut file." The cumulative experience of the FBI demonstrated that anonymous communications rarely contained any authentic information of value. Leads from identifiable, rational men and women were far more likely to be productive than those from phantom sources. The evaluator who failed to see the occasional nugget buried in the mail risked little chance of censure, for there was scant possibility that the oversight ever would be discovered. The evaluator who caused investigative resources to be squandered on leads that proved illusory would be faulted for poor judgment.

Still, from her days in Dallas, Janet remembered that the FBI there had ignored and thrown away a threatening letter received from Lee Harvey Oswald shortly before he assassinated President John F. Kennedy. So, tedious as work on the Complaint Desk often was, she took it seriously.

On the morning of May 11, 1984, Janet opened an anonymous typewritten letter addressed to "Agent in Charge, FBI, 450 Golden Gate Ave., San Francisco, CA 94118." She read the letter twice and tried to persuade herself that it should be consigned to the nut file. *The man has read too many spy stories. He's deluded himself into thinking he's a spy. Or he's playing a trick. He's trying to make us look silly. I'll look silly . . .*

Rejecting all of her own arguments, Janet took the elevator from the seventh to the sixth floor of the Federal Building, strode past the bulletproof glass of the reception room and through an electronically controlled door into the Soviet Section. There she searched out Special Agent John Peterson, handed him the letter, and said, "I feel this is something we ought to consider."

"Fine, Janet," he replied. "I'll take a look at it after lunch."

3

In a soft Southern accent, Janet Fournier implored, "John, read it right now."

Peterson started reading standing up, then sat down. The letter said:

Dear Sir:

I have been involved in espionage for several years, specifically, I've passed along Top Secret Cryptographic Keylists for military communications, Tech manuals for same, Intelligence Messages and etc.

I didn't know that the info was being passed to the U.S.S.R. until after I had been involved a few years, and since then I've been remorseful and wished to be free. Finally I've decided to stop supplying material — my contact doesn't know of my decision. Originally, I was told that I couldn't get out without approval, this was accompanied by threats. Since then, I believe the threats were a bluff.

At any rate, the reason for this letter is to give you (FBI) an opportunity to break what brobably [sic] is a significant espionage system. (I know that my contact has recurited [sic] at least three other members that are actively supplying highly classified material.) (I have the confidence of my contact.)

I pass the material to my contact (a U.S. citizen) who in turn passes the material to a contact overseas (his actual status — KGB or whatever — I don't know). That is not always the case tho, sometimes U.S. locations are used. A U.S. location is always used to receive instructions and money.

If you are interested in this matter, you can signal me with an ad in the Los Angeles *Times* classified section under "Personal messages (1225)." What I would expect to cooperate is *complete immunity* from prosecution and absolutely no public disclosure of me or my idenity [sic]. I will look for an ad in *Monday editions only* for the next four weeks. Also, I would desire some expense funds depending on the degree that my livelihood is interupted [sic].

The Ad: Start with "RUS:" followed by whatever message

4

you desire to pass. If your message is not clear, I'll send another letter. If I decide to cooperate, you will hear from me via an attorney. Otherwise nothing further will happen.

Sincerely,
RUS

Janet stayed until Peterson finished reading the letter. He stood up, offered her his hand, and said, "Thank you. I'll open a case immediately."

Peterson assigned the case to the man in whom he had the most confidence: himself. He promptly composed a response to RUS and then included its contents in an enciphered message informing FBI headquarters of the letter. Peterson did not ask permission to publish the reply and initiate an investigation. He simply told headquarters that that was what the San Francisco office intended to do "UACB" — "unless advised to the contrary by the bureau." "UACB" represented an impertinent yet usually effective bureaucratic ploy. Washington administrators easily could turn down a *request* without explaining; they could not halt an investigation already begun without putting themselves and their reasons on record.

Counterintelligence Supervisor William Smits was away for the day, and he had left Peterson in charge. So technically Peterson possessed authority to do what he did. Good form, though, would have dictated that he wait a few hours and consult the boss before starting a case, grabbing it for himself, and flashing a message to Washington. That he didn't hesitate surprised nobody in the office who really knew him.

Behind the façade of a rather handsome, expensively tailored and unfailingly polite FBI agent, John Peterson was an audacious man. The son of a physician, he had enjoyed an affluent childhood in Stockton, California, and he could have enjoyed a university education at his father's expense. But when he was twelve or thirteen, he saw the movie *Sands of Iwo Jima*, starring John Wayne as a courageous, selfless marine sergeant. From then on, Peterson knew exactly what he wanted to be: a U.S. Marine just like the one John Wayne portrayed. The summer after Peterson turned seventeen, his father took the family on a grand tour of Europe, then into the Soviet Union. John departed Moscow even more determined to be a marine. After one semester of college, in early 1966, he asked a recruiter if the Marine Corps could guarantee him duty as an infantryman in the front lines of Vietnam. Given the guarantee, he enlisted on the spot. He was eighteen.

Thirteen months of combat in Vietnam only fortified his faith in the cause that led him into the Marine Corps. He probably would have reenlisted had not his platoon commander convinced him that if he was to progress in the corps or anywhere else, he needed higher education.

During 1969, his freshman year at San Jose State, massive and often violent antiwar demonstrations raged on California campuses. Peterson applied to fourteen police departments for a job that would enable him to fight the demonstrators legally. Despite his war record and muscular physique, all rejected him because he stood only five feet seven inches, too short by their standards.

There was a professor he trusted, a former FBI agent, who pointed out that the bureau had a minimum height requirement of five feet seven. Abiding by his advice, Peterson joined the FBI as a clerk in Sacramento and continued his studies at night. After he received a degree in 1972, the FBI made him a full-fledged agent, sent him to Vietnamese language school for a year, then assigned him to counterintelligence. There, as in the Marine Corps and at college, Peterson looked for the best way to fight.

That night, May 11, 1984, Peterson stayed late at the office, smoking incessantly, sipping coffee, periodically pacing back and forth to invigorate himself. Dense fog enveloped the building and swirled low over the streets below, and he wondered if the Bay Bridge still would be passable. Again and again he read the letter, analyzing each sentence in quest of revelations about the author. He made a number of tentative deductions.

The envelope bore a Sacramento postmark. That, together with the fact that RUS elected to approach the San Francisco office, suggested that he probably lived in Northern California.

Keylists and *tech manuals* are arcane terms peculiar to cryptography. Peterson understood them only because during his early years as a clerk he had worked with FBI cipher machines. So RUS's indication that he had dealt with cryptographic materials was probably true.

Relatively few civilians have access to secret military communications, so the phantom author probably was a member of the armed forces.

Here, though, Peterson ran into a contradiction. For the reference to interruption of "livelihood" indicated that RUS did not receive the steady pay of a serviceman.

The redundant use of "and" before "etc.," the atrocious punctuation, misspellings, pedestrian wording, and disorganization of the letter reflected poor education. As most officers have a college education, RUS probably was not a commissioned officer.

RUS stated he had been involved in espionage "for several years" but claimed he did not realize he was serving the Soviet Union until after being involved "a few years." To Peterson, that meant that the "several" signified a good many years; six, seven, maybe more.

The length of involvement in turn suggested that if RUS was a military man, he was a mature regular rather than a youth serving an early enlistment.

The letter was a photocopy of a typewritten original. It is

almost impossible to scientifically match a photocopy with a particular typewriter. RUS knew something about conspiratorial ways. (Peterson suspected and the FBI laboratory later confirmed that the letter was bereft of fingerprints.)

Though he felt there was more to extract from the letter, Peterson gave up around midnight. He was too exhausted to think keenly, and in the morning he would have to face the Count.

Opinions as to why Bill Smits is called Count differ. Some say it is because he looks like a count — six feet two inches, slender and erect; thick steel-gray hair; aristocratic face; blue eyes alternately intimidating or encouraging. Others argue the title sticks because of his mannerisms; urbane, in the view of many; imperious, according to detractors.

Smits always had detractors. Peterson, admittedly a partisan, dismissed them all. They did not speak Russian and German fluently; they did not have a Ph.D.; their doctoral dissertation was not adjudged one of the most definitive studies of Soviet theft of Western technology. None of the critics had ever run a real case or caught a major spy or recruited a Soviet or handled an important defector. "Count never climbed over the back of anyone," Peterson had declared a few months before in briefing a newly arrived agent. "He got where he is on his own."

The next morning, Smits's corner office looked to Peterson like the dormitory room of a college sophomore who always means to straighten up after the next exams, a veritable rat's nest of charts, reference books, encyclopedias, dictionaries, files, reports. There was even a large photograph of a sultry, voluptuous girl in a bikini; it was inscribed "Merry Christmas to the boys on the Squad, Lulu." The only neat space was around the computer with which Smits spent much of his time.

Realizing that Peterson would not barge in without an appointment frivolously, Smits took the letter and read it at once. Putting it down, he noncommittally asked, "Where did you get this?"

"Janet spotted it."

"Talk to her. Tell her to mention it to no one. If we hear from him again, she is to come straight to you, or to me if you are away," Smits ordered. He instructed his secretary to deflect calls and visitors, closed his door, and returned to the letter.

Emerging from hibernation around noon, Smits surprised Peterson with an invitation to lunch at the Mark Hopkins Hotel. Smits disliked long lunches, preferring to have a sandwich while playing chess in the park or reading newspapers at his desk. And the old Mark Hopkins, towering atop Nob Hill, was a hard twenty-minute walk away, mostly uphill.

Once there, Smits astonished Peterson further by leading him into the lobby bar, a grand salon with a domed ceiling of opaque glass. Except for two matrons sipping tea, it was deserted, and they sequestered themselves on a sofa behind a corner table. From an uncommonly pretty waitress attired in a tight skirt, Smits ordered a disgusting concoction of Irish whiskey and cream. But it was a drink, and Smits almost never drank alcohol. Peterson ordered an Anchor Steam beer and wondered if perhaps his boss was observing some secret anniversary, maybe remembering a former love he had known at the Mark.

In fact, Smits ceremonially was observing the onset of what he sensed to be the case of his career. It was a career filled with big cases, a career that began in secret communications, cryptography, and cryptanalysis. Bored by college, Smits had dropped out in 1957 and enlisted in the army as a private. Because of his extraordinary intelligence test scores, the army assigned him to intelligence; he was intensively trained as a Russian linguist and posted to Germany. For two years he listened to Soviet radio broadcasts and learned about ciphers, how to protect them as well as how to break them. After he left the army and completed college, the FBI employed him as an agent, and he spent two and a half years teaching FBI agents the Russian language. Years later as legal attaché in the U.S. embassy in Bonn, he again worked with cipher machines and cryptographic materials.

Peterson saw the implications of the RUS letter as grave; Smits, given his experience in cryptography, saw them as possibly catastrophic. The technical manuals necessary to maintain and repair cipher machines minutely detail the components, circuitry, and logic of the machines. If the KGB, the Soviet espionage apparatus, had acquired technical manuals from RUS, then Soviet experts could build exact duplicates of American cipher machines. Keylists in effect are ciphers, which change daily. If the Soviets had both the cipher machines and the keylists, they could read the most secret American communications just as easily as could Americans themselves.

In the ramblings of RUS, Smits also saw the outline of a classic espionage network presided over by a principal agent, the "contact." The principal agent acted as a middleman, collecting from the producers, subagents such as RUS, and delivering to the customer, the Soviet Union. He himself did not require direct access to secrets. He could be any obscure person employed in any position that afforded plausible pretext to travel at will. His suppliers need never risk exposure by meeting a Russian. He deposited their product in remote hiding places, "drops," and from similar places gathered funds and instructions. Few face-to-face meetings between him and the KGB would be necessary. And they would occur only outside the country, most likely in Mexico or Austria, beyond the normal reach of the FBI.

To Smits, these tradecraft procedures were elementary and familiar; the Soviets had employed them for more than sixty years. But all KGB operations in the United States heretofore observed by him involved only a lone American agent. Not since discovery of the spy ring that stole Anglo-American secrets of the atomic bomb had the FBI encountered a Soviet network.

If RUS could be believed, despite his claimed retirement, the rest of the network remained intact, hard and successfully at work. The danger had not passed; it was clear and present. And the danger was all the greater because it originated from multiple and mutually supportive sources.

"Who is RUS?" Smits asked, putting the question as much to himself as to Peterson.

He listened closely as Peterson recited his earlier deductions and the rationale for them. "Of course, that's all conjecture," Peterson concluded. "I may be wrong about everything."

"Unfortunately, you probably are right about almost everything," Smits replied. "If so, we're dealing with one squalid, selfish cretin. He's been selling out his country for years. Now he's considering selling out his partners, all for himself. He pretends to be remorseful. Yet he doesn't want to suffer in the least for his sins. He wants us to forget about his treason, to cover it up, to cleanse his conscience, to say, 'Thanks, fellow American. Well done. Go in peace and live happily ever after. And by the way, do enjoy all the money the KGB gave you.' Not only that; the son of a bitch wants us to pay him to atone! He's a sociopath, unrestrained by any morals or ideals whatsoever. But he's dangerous because, obviously, he's functional and effective."

"Then you think the letter is authentic?" Peterson asked.

"There are many more reasons to believe than to disbelieve," Smits answered. "It won't hurt to secure a second opinion from Miron. Meanwhile, let's try to make RUS show his face."

After cheeseburgers in the downstairs coffee shop, they started back. The northern and eastern approaches to the Federal Building form a transitional area of the city. Prized old apartments, sleek new structures, and colorful little ethnic cafés coexist with massage parlors, homosexual theaters, porno shops, and dark bars fit only for troglodytes.

As they walked along, a man loitering on the corner briskly called to them, "Hey, fellows, can you spare some change? I'm hungry. I'd like to get myself some macaroni and cheese." He looked hale, healthy, quite sober, and under thirty.

"We don't believe in that," Smits snapped.

Sheepishly, the vagrant retreated and said, "Yeah, I know what you mean."

Farther on, an aged alcoholic cloaked in a strip of dirty burlap thrust a palsied hand in their faces, silently begging. Beneath white whiskers, bloated skin sagged from his face; saliva leaked from the corner of his mouth; his few teeth were stained yellow and brown. Smits gave him five dollars.

"You schizoid?"

"He can't help himself; the other one can."

Suddenly Peterson muttered, "Goddammit!" He stepped quickly in front of Smits and parted his jacket to make the revolver in his shoulder holster more accessible.

Having rounded the street corner, eight or nine young men now bore down on them. They wore obscene leotards, shirts open to the navel, necklaces, bracelets, earrings, filthy hair knotted in trailing braids. Glazed eyes betrayed the deranging effect of drugs, which eroded the restraint of reason and fear. And they were in a pack.

"Control yourself, John."

Peterson planted himself in the center of the sidewalk, hand inside his jacket. He returned their leers with an unflinching stare, and the gang separated, passing on either side without incident.

"This is a fucking zoo," Peterson grumbled.

"Think about RUS," Smits said royally as he rebuttoned his own jacket. "We've got a job to do."

Murray S. Miron is one of the nation's foremost practitioners of psycholinguistics, the art of characterizing an individual by analysis of his or her speech and writings. Although psycholinguistics has not been widely accepted as a science, Miron's analyses had been useful to the FBI in the past, and some had proved to be remarkably prescient. Trusting Miron's discretion and integrity, Smits that afternoon arranged for delivery of a copy of the letter to him at the Psycholinguistics Center in Rochester, New York.

On Monday, May 21, 1984, a terse notice appeared among the classified advertisements in the *Los Angeles Times:* "RUS: Considering your offer. Call weekdays 9 a.m.–11 a.m. 415/626-2793 or write ME, SF."

The number listed was that of a special telephone newly installed on Peterson's desk. Any call received on it would be instantly traced. But the phone did not ring on Monday or Tuesday. Paradoxically, Peterson in a way hoped it would not ring. If the FBI ad elicited no reaction, then one reasonably could argue that RUS was a pretender, that the letter was a hoax, and that the perils it conjured up were unreal. Peterson even suggested this possibility to Smits, who glanced at him quizzically, like a professor regarding a gifted pupil who momentarily had lapsed into fatuity.

In any case, such wishful conjecture on the morning of May 23 became moot. Janet Fournier recognized the letter at once because the typewritten address was the same as on the first.

Having waited a few minutes to subdue her excitement, she went through the electronic door, passed through a narrow corridor lined with tiny offices, and crossed a wide, open area with many desks, which resembled the newsroom of a metropolitan paper. She located Peterson in his cubbyhole, gave him the unopened letter, and said, "I think this is what you've been waiting for."

"Well, why didn't you open it?"

"Maybe it's very important. Maybe I have no need to know."

Peterson fumbled through his desk drawer for a pair of surgical rubber gloves and with difficulty slipped them on. He sliced open the envelope, made a copy of the letter for himself and another for Smits, then placed the original in a safe.

In Smits's office, the two men read their copies of the letter.

Dear Sir:

I saw your note today and was encouraged, however, I'm not going to call for obvious reasons. I'll admit that my most earnest desire is to talk to someone (like yourself) about my situation, but I feel that I'm unable to trust any kind of personal contact — phone included. Nor have I begun to look for an attorney. Where does that leave us or more specifically me?

I'll be very open. It took me several months to finally write the first letter. Yes, I'm remorseful, and I feel that to come forward and help break the espionage ring would compensate for my wrong doing [sic], consequently clearing my conscience. But there are other emotions: the difficulty of ratting on a "friend" and the potential of getting caught up in a legal mess (public disclosure of my involvement and a possible double-cross on immunity, assuming it was granted in the first place).

I would guess that you are conferring with higher authority and possibly other agencies. I'm wondering if my situation is really considered serious enough to warrant investigation and to give me due consideration (immunity and etc.)!

14

I'm going to begin looking for an attorney, which will be tricky from my view, to discuss my situation. And I will keep an eye on the LA Times, Monday editions, for any additional word/instructions from you.

It certainly would be nice for people in my predicament to have a means of confidential consultation with someone in a position of authority without the possibility of arrest.

My contact will be expecting more material from me in a few months, if I don't I'm not sure what his response will be. I'm going to come clean with him at that time (assuming no deal is made with you) and tell him I'm finished with the "business." And then get on with my life.

More info on him: He has been in "the business" for more than 20 years and plans to continue indefinitely. He thinks he has a good organization and has no real fear of being caught, less some coincidental misfortune; in that regard he feels safe also. I agree with his assessment.

Why haven't I discussed my desire to come clean (with you) with my contact and/or possibly convince him to do the same? It would be sure folly — dangerous to my health.

Sincerely,
RUS

One phrase leaped up at them — "He has been in 'the business' for more than 20 years." In modern espionage few if any spies, much less entire nets, had survived undetected, let alone unsuspected, for as long as twenty years. If the Soviets had broken into secret American communications, the resultant volume of intelligence would be staggering. Its processing would demand the full time of hundreds of KGB analysts. Unavoidable personnel turnover through the years would multiply the number of people with some knowledge that the KGB was reading enciphered American messages.

During the preceding twenty years the CIA, FBI, the British, and the French had recruited ranking KGB officers, then maintained them as agents in place both at Moscow head-

15

quarters and Soviet embassies abroad. Other KGB officers had jumped unexpectedly to the West. Yet the vast amounts of often invaluable data they collectively supplied contained not a hint of the kind of operation in which RUS claimed to be a participant.

A KGB colonel upon his defection to the United States in 1983 did report that the KGB had one great operation whose importance eclipsed all others throughout the world. But he had no idea of its nature. He could offer only the suspicion that two officers he named were involved, because both, at different times, had been spectacularly promoted from middle grades to the rank of general. Both had served in Washington. Seemingly, though, neither ever did anything unusual outside the embassy, and because of their passivity the FBI put them down as administrators or technicians.

How could the KGB totally conceal an operation of such magnitude for so long?

Reflecting aloud, Smits remarked, "Department Sixteen just might be able to pull it off. Certainly, it would be a Department Sixteen case." He asked Peterson, "Have you ever talked to Stan about Sixteen?"

Peterson shook his head.

Stan was Stanislav Levchenko, a KGB major who had fled from Tokyo to the United States in late 1979. Smits loved to talk shop with Levchenko, to look at espionage from the Soviet perspectives he could provide, to discover little details Levchenko had forgotten or never been asked about. Once they had talked about Department 16, which is responsible for subverting foreign cipher and communications personnel.

Department 16, Levchenko explained, is one of the two most secret components of the KGB, the other being the department responsible for assassinations. The KGB keeps Department 16 officers in Moscow, hidden from hostile counterintelligence services, and all cipher cases are managed from headquarters. If an officer must venture abroad to meet a source, the rendezvous occurs in a neutral or Third World country the Soviets consider safe. Even so, the KGB may dispatch an elite team from the Surveillance Directorate in Moscow to safeguard the meeting. At headquarters, an officer supervises but one case. All operational records pertaining to it are kept in a safe that only he can unlock in an office only he may enter.

The same rules of secrecy and compartmentation apply in the field. An officer requisitioned from another KGB department to locate and service drops in furtherance of Department 16 operations performs no other clandestine tasks. He scrupulously lives his cover at the embassy and does nothing to merit attention from counterintelligence. He even appears to colleagues to be doing nothing and may slip out to load and unload drops no more than two or three times a year.

Summarizing Levchenko's confidences, Smits said, "You see, it's just possible."

Peterson replied, "RUS said he has been involved for several years. How could he know that his contact has been spying for more than twenty?"

"I suppose the contact told him."

"Maybe the contact lied or exaggerated. Maybe RUS is lying or exaggerating."

"Maybe. But there is a disturbing consistency and logic in the two letters."

In the first letter, Smits pointed out, RUS claimed he enjoyed the confidence of his contact; in the second he referred to him as a "friend." RUS in both letters betrayed the kind of intimate knowledge of the network and its modus operandi the contact would have imparted only to a trusted friend or associate. A trained KGB officer would never commit such security breaches. So the contact probably was, as RUS said, an American.

The flagrant security breaches by the contact meant that the KGB did not and could not completely control his conduct of the operation in the United States. Yet both letters indicated that the Soviets for many, many years had continued "the business" with him. They would not have done so unless he delivered value. So the contact probably was a very able, self-assured freebooter. Having succeeded for so long, he naturally would think he could succeed indefinitely.

Peterson admired and accepted the reasoning, but he never complimented Smits except behind his back. He said only, "We still don't know any more than we did about RUS."

"Yes, we do. RUS is real. His story, in essence, is true."

The FBI responded to the second RUS letter with an advertisement in the June 4 edition of the *Los Angeles Times:* "RUS: Understand your concerns, but we can help. Must have dialogue with you or proxy, if you are serious. ME, SF."

That morning and each thereafter, Janet Fournier pounced on the mail; Peterson sat unmoving by the special telephone; Smits, alone in his office, brooded and thought. *We must smoke him out. We must talk to him. Everything depends upon finding this one miserable man.*

Hearing nothing, Smits and Peterson devised a desperate stratagem manifested in an advertisement that appeared Monday, June 11:

RUS: Considering your dilemma. Need to speak to you to see what I can do. This can be done anonymously. Just you and me at 10 a.m. June 21 at intersection of the street of my office and Hyde Street in my city. I'll carry a newspaper in my left hand. We will only discuss your situation to provide you with guidance as to where you stand. No action will be taken against you whatsoever at this meeting. Respond if you cannot make it or if you want to change locations. I want to help you in your very trying situation, but I need facts to be able to assist you.

At 10:00 A.M. on June 21, Peterson lingered at the corner of Golden Gate Avenue and Hyde Street, a newspaper in his left hand. Disguised FBI surveillants ringed the area, and overhead a light aircraft, outfitted with secret communications and observation equipment, lazily circled.

The critical words in the ad were "at this meeting." Bound by them, the FBI did not intend to arrest RUS. It did intend to follow him and ascertain his identity. RUS, however, did not appear.

When Peterson returned to the office, Smits showed him an undated memorandum that Janet had brought a few minutes earlier.

FM: RUS
TO: Agent in Charge
      FBI, San Francisco
Sir:
   I won't be meeting you the 21st. A letter will follow in a week or two.

While daily awaiting the promised letter, Smits received Murray Miron's psycholinguistic analysis of the first letter. It should have been professionally pleasing; instead, it disheartened him. Dr. Miron wrote:

This report is based upon material classified, in part, as SECRET and should be handled accordingly.

This communication exhibits a number of characteristics which suggest that it should be considered to be highly credible. It is quite likely that anyone engaged in espionage would be expected, on *a priori* grounds if no other, to be psychopathic in character. Idealists who might try to aid or abet our enemies would be expected to eschew any money for themselves so as to better prove their "nobler" intentions. The author of this letter exhibits the language of the psychopath. His passing reference to conscience is both glib and superficial. Even the protestation of remorse is mitigated by the notion that the author wishes to be free of what we can presume to be some pressures consequent of an earlier attempt to demur from further participation. The author's psychopathic bent is further supported by his ending request that he be compensated for "interruption" of his "livelihood." All of this is entirely believable.

Based upon the content and style of the author's language, it is my judgment that he is a technically trained Caucasian male approximately between the ages of 30 and 45. There are indications that the author is familiar with cryptography, codes and radio/computer apparatus. Although he is, in my judgment, clearly psychopathic, he can be expected to be sufficiently shrewd and wily to have avoided detection for other schemes in which he may be involved; i.e., he would not be expected to have a criminal record and (would be expected) to have received relatively high fitness reports on his job.

Although personally convinced that the RUS letters were authentic, Smits nevertheless allowed for the possibility that he was wrong; that the congenital suspicions and mindset of a professional counterintelligence officer might have skewed his judgment. Miron had seen only the first letter and was unaware of subsequent exchanges. Working with far less information and from a completely different professional background, he had reached the same essential conclusion as had Smits and Peterson. If there had been any excuses for not going ahead, Miron's analysis swept them away. But where should they look?

Through late June and into early August RUS remained mute. With an advertisement published August 13, the FBI tried anew to coax him out of the shadows. "RUS: Haven't heard from you, still want to meet. Propose meeting in Ensenada, Mexico, a neutral site. If you need travel funds, will furnish same at your choice of location in Silicon Valley or anywhere else. Please respond to the above."

Two days later Janet handed Peterson a response.

August 13, 1984

RUS
Somewhere, U.S.A.
Agent in Charge
FBI
450 Golden Gate Ave.
San Francisco, CA 94118
Dear Sir:

I saw your note in todays [sic] LA Times. Since my last note to you, I've done a lot of serious thinking and have pretty much come to the conclusion that it would be best to give up on the idea of aiding in the termination of the espionage ring previously discussed.

To think I could help you and not make my own involvement known to the public I believe is naive. Nor have I contacted an attorney. I have great difficulty in coming forth, particularly since the chances of my past involvement ever being known is [sic] extremenely [sic] remote as long as I remain silent.

Yes, I can still say I would prefer to get it off my chest, to come clean.

The above notwithstanding, I'll think about a meeting in Ensenada. Funds are not the problem.

My contact is pressing for more material, but so far no real problems have occurred. I haven't explicitly told him I'm no longer in the business.

Sincerely,
[unsigned]

Smits recalled another conversation with Levchenko, this one about agents who spy solely for money. "Sooner or later, the mercenary will begin to vacillate and become erratic," Levchenko said. "When that happens, you know he is thinking about quitting. Many times he actually will quit because he's afraid or feels guilty. In such cases, the KGB knows to be patient. Decades of experience show that eventually he will go back to work because he's addicted to the money. If he doesn't come back, that usually means he's been caught."

RUS long had vacillated. He vacillated for months before writing the first letter. He planned to engage a lawyer but made no attempt to find one. He intended to inform his contact that he was quitting the ring, but he did not. Now he had "pretty much" decided not to cooperate with the FBI, yet he still toyed with the possibility of doing so.

"I doubt that he will really quit," Smits said. "And I very much doubt we will hear from him again." It happened that on both counts Smits was right.

Peterson stayed on the case and uncovered two suspects who seemed to approximate the profile drawn of RUS. Both were military men, one recently retired, the other still on active duty. Discreet investigation disclosed no grounds for suspecting either of any wrongdoing. In early October Peterson reported that all trails had turned cold, and he had no more leads.

Smits observed, "There's an epigram that reads, 'God looks after fools, drunkards, and the United States.' I hope so. They're into our communications, and we're in trouble." But he had no proof.

2

Something Is Wrong

LOOKING BACK, we can see now that through the years there were many signs that something was wrong.

Having delivered a lecture about security at the National Defense Institute in Washington, FBI agent David Major fell into conversation with a navy admiral. The admiral mentioned that no matter how strict the secrecy, whenever the navy staged a large exercise, Soviet ships were always waiting in the operational area. "It is as if they had a copy of the OpPlans [operational plans]. Something is wrong."

Signs were apparent in the last stage of the Vietnam War. Theodore Shackly, a retired Central Intelligence Agency officer who was station chief in Saigon from 1968 to 1973, recalls: "They usually had forewarning of the B-52 strikes. Even when the B-52s diverted to secondary targets because of weather, they knew in advance which targets would be hit. Naturally, the foreknowledge diminished the effectiveness of the strikes because they were ready. It was uncanny. We never figured it out."

Throughout the 1960s and 1970s the United States enjoyed a decisive superiority over the Soviet Union in the technology of submarine warfare. The U.S. Navy easily tracked noisy Soviet submarines throughout the oceans of the world. Wherever they sailed, they were always at risk because the navy had them in its sights. But in the late 1970s and early 1980s, new Soviet submarines took to the seas. They were almost as quiet as the latest American submarines. The Soviets had apparently discovered in precise detail the ultrasecret American means of trailing them and by redesign frustrated those means. How did they make the discoveries?

Soviet submarines started lurking off Guam, Holy Loch, Rota, La Madalena, and Pacific Coast bases, waiting to follow U.S. missile submarines when they sortied. By evasive tactics, the Americans always lost the pursuers without much trouble, although the necessity of maneuvering off course did add as much as a day to already lengthy patrols. Operationally, the Soviet actions were little more than a nuisance, but they implied foreknowledge of just when U.S. submarines would leave port, which was troubling.

The U.S. Navy in 1983 dispatched an exceptionally powerful battle group, including three aircraft carriers, on an exercise off the Kamchatka Peninsula of the Soviet Union. A principal purpose was to gauge Soviet reaction to the approach of such a formidable flotilla. The Soviets scarcely reacted at all. Again, as the admiral said, it was as if they possessed a copy of the operational plan, as if they understood exactly what the navy was attempting.

The trouble was not confined to the navy. Prime Minister Maurice Bishop of Grenada in 1979 accused the United States of plotting to overthrow his government. Inured to baseless communist charges of imperialist plots and imminent aggression, the world ignored Bishop. But the relatively few persons privy to National Security Council deliberations winced because this time there was some truth in the allegations.

The most conspicuous indication that something was very wrong should have been recognized in the autumn of 1980. The preceding April a U.S. raid to free fifty-two Americans in

Iran foundered ignominiously in the desert. Humiliated and seemingly impotent, the Carter administration laid plans to redeem itself in the eyes of the electorate by mounting a much larger attack upon Iran. During the summer preparations proceeded in unprecedented secrecy. By September the United States had deployed a strike force consisting of five thousand assault troops and ten thousand reserves who could be landed quickly in Iran if needed.

With equal secrecy, the Soviet Union moved twenty-two full divisions to the Iranian border. They included at least two airborne divisions and a KGB division responsible for security and communications. To support them the Soviets additionally repositioned reconnaissance and communications satellites. They were all ready, just waiting.

American reconnaissance detected the poised Soviet formations. With their discovery, a horrendous specter immediately became apparent: The moment the U.S. raiders land, the Soviets invoke an old mutual assistance treaty with Iran. Soviet airborne troops quickly surround the Americans, while Soviet armored divisions hurtle across the border. They come not as occupiers but as protectors of Islam against the satanic American aggressors. President Carter now must choose. He can let the vastly outnumbered American force surrender or be annihilated. Or he can resort to nuclear weapons and risk precipitating World War III.

Prudently, Carter canceled the raid.

The Soviet divisions did not appear on the frontier overnight. They were massed gradually over a period of several weeks. Thus, the Soviets obviously had considerable advance warning of highly secret American plans. How did they know? The question was never answered.

No single person saw all of these signs as they popped up at different times and places over the years. Hence, no one could have suspected that they all might be warning of the same calamity: Soviet penetration of American communications. Besides, as everyone familiar with them understood, enciphered American communications basically were impenetrable.

American military and diplomatic communications, of course, are under incessant attack. From the towers standing across the Soviet Union and its satellites, including Cuba; from electronics-laden trawlers lazing off the North American coasts and tagging along after U.S. fleets; from diplomatic installations in Washington, New York, and San Francisco, the Russians endeavor to intercept and record all secret American messages. And no matter where a message originates — *Air Force One,* the National Command Center, the White House, the Pentagon, a shuttle in space, a destroyer or aircraft carrier on tumultuous seas, a submarine patrolling silently beneath the ocean, a formation of fighter aircraft pursuing terrorists over the Mediterranean, embassies abroad — it must be assumed that the Soviets have taped it in the hope of someday deciphering it.

Despite this continuing assault, confidence in the unbreakability of American cipher systems remained undaunted, and indeed, the systems are wondrous creations.*

A cipher system consists of two fundamental components known as the logic and the keys. The logic, an ultrapowerful algorithm, or mathematical formula, is embodied in the transistor, or microcircuitry, of an electronic machine. An operator types a plain-language message into the machine, which almost instantly translates it into a garbled form unintelligible

---

*Popularly and even among professionals, the words *codes* and *ciphers* are used interchangeably. Strictly speaking, there is a difference. In a code, letters, numerals, or words stand for a particular word, phrase, complete sentence, or entire thought. In a cipher, letters or numerals or groups of them represent individual letters or numerals.

to anyone not equipped with a machine containing the same logic. (Machines designed to encrypt voice communications or transmissions from computer to computer naturally are without a typewriter keyboard.)

In the simplest of ciphers, a letter or numeral or group of them represents another letter or numeral. But a modern cipher machine makes possible millions of variations. For example, in a message the letter *e,* the most recurrent in English, might appear one hundred times. The logic will ensure that in the garbled text transmitted, the letters or numerals signifying *e* never are the same. The possible permutations are so vast that, in theory, no cryptanalyst studying messages so enciphered can divine the underlying logic and thereby lay bare their meaning.

The keys make the system even more inscrutable by altering the functioning of the logic and the starting point of the logic process. Keys come in the form of cards, paper tapes, or lists of numbers. The perforated cards or tapes may be inserted directly into a machine or into a card reader, which is placed in the machine; the numbers on a keylist provide directions for manual setting of the machine. In whichever form, the key revises the encryption process. Keys normally are changed every twenty-four hours, and consequently the machine internally works differently each day. Thus, in theory, no one can decipher an encrypted American message without possessing both the logic of the machine and the one key for the precise period in which the message was encrypted. And once a key is used, it is destroyed.

All American cipher systems and cryptographic materials are designed, engineered, produced, or printed by the National Security Agency at Fort Meade, Maryland, outside Washington. The NSA subjects each job applicant to an exhaustive background investigation and polygraph examination. Employees periodically are reinvestigated and tested by polygraph. Despite the necessary forfeiture of privacy, people of the highest caliber continue to apply to work at the NSA.

Among them are many of the nation's most gifted scientists, mathematicians, engineers, and scholars. They carry on a national tradition of cryptography and cryptanalysis unmatched by any other nation save possibly Great Britain. They work with the most advanced computer in the world, the Cray, which no other nation has. And one division of the NSA does nothing but continuously assess, practically and theoretically, the vulnerabilities of the systems they create.

The NSA imposes upon all governmental and military users the most stringent rules governing the handling and safeguarding of cryptographic materials. As a result, a cipher machine, set of keys, or technical manual is continuously and physically accounted for from the time it is produced until the moment it is destroyed in the field or returned to Fort Meade. And, as they say in the military, "If you want a quick visit from your commanding officer, just mishandle crypto."

The United States expends inordinate effort and hundreds of millions of dollars annually to preserve the sanctity of its communications, because a serious breach of them can mean, literally, the death of a nation. The implications of the RUS letters so alarmed Smits, Peterson, and others in the FBI because they keenly comprehended this stark fact. Smits especially understood, because during his studies of cryptography he had learned the deadly lessons of recent history.

Most Americans under the age of fifty have difficulty visualizing their country as it was before World War II. The United States in 1940 had a population of 132 million, and the entire U.S. Armed Forces totaled 458,000 men. Japan had more than 4 million men under arms, and many were veterans of combat in China, with which Japan had been at war since 1937. American military equipment, notably naval fighter aircraft, torpedo bombers, and torpedoes themselves, often were markedly inferior to Japanese weaponry. American productive, technological, and organizational genius eventually would assert itself. But in each of the early, great battles that doomed Japan, American forces were outnumbered by a better-equipped and far more experienced enemy.

The United States did have one advantage. In 1940 a brilliant team of cryptanalysts succeeded in constructing an analogue, or replica, of the principal Japanese cipher machine. Henceforth, the United States was able to decrypt messages transmitted in the Japanese diplomatic cipher. The breakthrough eventually led to the unraveling of Japanese naval and merchant marine ciphers. Additionally, navy analysts had learned to squeeze priceless intelligence even from secret Japanese radio communications that at the time could not be decrypted.

The most decisive battle of the Pacific war was fought around the tiny island of Midway less than six months after the Japanese shattered the U.S. Fleet at Pearl Harbor. In May 1942 the Japanese put to sea the most formidable naval armada ever assembled up until that time. It confidently advanced upon Midway, determined to seize the island and lure the remnants of U.S. naval forces into a grand fleet action that would result in their annihilation. Then nothing would stand between the Japanese and Hawaii or California, and occupation of Midway would seal a strategic ring around the approaches to Japan.

On the eve of battle, the odds against the United States seemed hopeless. Nobody has more eloquently summed them up than historian Walter Lord. In the foreword to his book *Incredible Victory* he wrote:

By any ordinary standard, they were hopelessly outclassed.
They had no battleships, the enemy eleven. They had eight
cruisers, the enemy twenty-three. They had three carriers (one
of them crippled); the enemy had eight. Their shore defense
included guns from the turn of the century.

They knew little of war. None of the Navy pilots on one of
their carriers had ever been in combat. Nor had any of the
Army fliers. Of the Marines, 17 of 21 new pilots were just out
of flight school — some with less than four hours' flying time
since then. Their enemy was brilliant, experienced and all-
conquering.

They were tired, dead tired. The patrol plane crews, for in-
stance, had been flying 15 hours a day, servicing their own
planes, getting perhaps three hours' sleep at night.

They had equipment problems. Some of their dive bombers
couldn't dive — the fabric came off the wings. Their torpedoes
were slow and unreliable; the torpedo planes even worse. Yet
they were up against the finest fighting plane in the world.

They took crushing losses — 15 out of 15 in one torpedo
squadron . . . 21 out of 27 in a group of fighters . . . many,
many more.

They had no right to win. Yet they did, and in doing so they
changed the course of a war. More than that, they added a new
name — Midway — to that small list that inspires by shining
example. Like Marathon, the Armada, the Marne, a few others, Midway showed that every once in a while "what must be"
need not be at all. Even against the greatest of odds, there is
something in the human spirit — a magic blend of skill, faith
and valor — that can lift men from certain defeat to incredible
victory.

Nothing can subtract from the valor of the American pilots,
most in their early twenties, who fought and died around Midway in combat against equally brave adversaries. Nothing can
diminish the brilliance of admirals Chester Nimitz and
Raymond Spruance, who planned and executed American ac-

30

tions at Midway. However, no amount of individual courage or professional genius could have produced the "incredible victory" had not the Americans broken into Japanese communications.

By spring 1942 navy cryptanalysts at Pearl Harbor had begun to read parts of messages transmitted in the Japanese naval cipher JN25B. On the average, they could understand no more than 10 to 12 percent of a given text. But combined with direction finding, analysis of the origins and volume of Japanese transmissions, and their general knowledge of the Japanese fleet, this proved enough. They pieced together a comprehensive and stunningly accurate picture of the Japanese battle plan, which showed Nimitz virtually all he needed to know. As British historian Ronald Lewin wrote in his masterful work *The American Magic,* "Nimitz, on the eve of his next great battle, had a more intimate knowledge of his enemy's strength and intentions than any other admiral in the whole previous history of sea warfare."

Given this foreknowledge, Nimitz did everything right. He concentrated all available ships for the battle, compelling the badly damaged carrier *Yorktown* in two days to be made seaworthy, if not fully battle worthy. The Japanese planned to employ seaplanes, refueled from submarines at the empty French Frigate Shoals, to watch the American fleet at Pearl Harbor. Nimitz denied them such reconnaissance by stationing ships at French Frigate Shoals to prevent the refueling. He then slipped his ships out of Pearl Harbor before Japanese submarines arrived to form a reconnaissance cordon. The Japanese thus did not know where the ships were. He knew where theirs were, thanks to the cryptanalysts.

The Japanese planned to fragment American forces by sending a feinting flotilla toward the Aleutians. Nimitz ignored the ruse.

Nimitz so heavily fortified Midway that it withstood the first

Japanese air strike. Despite serious losses, the defenders remained capable of inflicting heavy casualties on any invaders. Consequently, the Japanese recognized the necessity of a second strike against the atoll, a necessity that was to prove fatal.

Certainly, the first phase of the battle did nothing to erode their confidence or arrogance. Despite outrageously false claims subsequently issued from General Douglas MacArthur's headquarters, army bombers flying from Midway hit not a single ship. The old, lumbering navy torpedo planes may have scored a few hits; if so, none of their torpedoes exploded, and almost all the planes were shot down. And Japanese Zeroes slaughtered antique American fighters.

Then everything changed. From the carriers *Enterprise* and *Hornet* Spruance launched every remaining aircraft. The decks of the four heavy carriers in the Japanese strike force, *Akagi, Kaga, Soryu,* and *Hiryu,* were congested with planes, fuel, bombs, and ammunition as sailors feverishly prepared for the second attack on Midway. Suddenly a lookout shouted, "Helldivers!" In minutes, U.S. dive-bombers transformed *Kaga, Soryu,* and *Akagi* into sinking charnel houses.

Hours later, planes from the surviving *Hiryu* sank the *Yorktown,* which had been further crippled by torpedoes from a Japanese submarine. Most of the *Yorktown* crew, however, was saved. And the next day, pilots from the *Enterprise* and *Hornet* eliminated *Hiryu.* Bereft of air power, the Japanese armada retreated to Japan.

In addition to the four carriers and some cruisers and destroyers, the Japanese navy at Midway lost more than 300 aircraft and the elite of its flight crews. More important, it lost a spirit and élan that never were recovered.

In early 1943 American cryptanalysts broke the cipher used to organize and direct convoys of Japanese merchant ships.

No longer did U.S. submarines have to grope about the vast expanses of the Pacific hoping for chance encounters. From deciphered instructions, they knew not only the routes of merchant convoys but precisely where a convoy would be each day at noon, and they had only to lie in wait. Massive destruction of the merchant marine began to sap the very lifeblood of Japan while strangling many of its far-off outposts. Japan started the war with some 6 million tons of merchant shipping. U.S. submarines alone sank more than 4.7 million tons, and aircraft, also guided by decrypts, accounted for added tonnage.

But the most profound consequences of American ability to read Japanese communications cannot be observed in the history of any one battle or sphere of operations, however important. For the consequences were strategic and transcendent. The fact is that encyclopedic, authentic knowledge of Japanese strengths, weaknesses, and intentions, extracted almost daily from their own words, largely conditioned the overall American conduct of the war in the Pacific from Midway to Hiroshima. Without that knowledge, the war surely would have continued much longer, and countless more human beings of all nationalities would have perished.

The same was true in Europe. If possible, the reading of enemy communications even more decisively affected the war there.

Polish intelligence in 1939 delivered to the British the basic German cipher machine, Enigma. By spring 1940 a gifted British team laboring at Bletchley Park, an estate outside London, mastered its functions sufficiently to begin reading some German ciphers, particularly those of the Luftwaffe.

After the fall of France, the Luftwaffe undertook to destroy the Royal Air Force preparatory to a cross-channel invasion by the Wehrmacht. Standing alone, clinging precariously to life in face of German might, the British trusted their fate to a few hundred young pilots and their Spitfires and Hurricanes. But they and their great commander, Air Chief Marshal Hugh Dowding, had a silent ally in the cryptanalysts.

In the Battle of Britain, beginning July 10, 1940, they often alerted Dowding as to the time, composition, and strategic purpose of forthcoming German raids. Intercepts, for example, revealed that the Luftwaffe had designated August 15 as *Adler Tag,* or Eagle Day, a day on which its massive formations would entice all British fighters into the sky and wipe them out in one fell swoop. Aware of both German strategy and tactics on *Adler Tag,* Dowding artfully directed and husbanded his planes and won the day. The Luftwaffe lost seventy-five aircraft, the RAF thirty-four. Unable to sustain such losses, the Germans tacitly admitted defeat, canceled the planned invasion (an act Bletchley Park promptly reported), and resorted to night bombing of British cities.

The skill and intrepidity of the British pilots, the quality of their aircraft, the excellence of British radar, the flawless generalship of Dowding, made possible the victory that saved Great Britain. But the cryptanalysts made a significant contribution, and in a battle so narrowly won, any significant factor may be said to have been crucial.

German naval ciphers defied the British until May 1941. Under attack off Greenland, the crew of *U-110* abandoned the submarine, setting explosives timed to scuttle it. The explosives, however, failed to detonate. Rowing through heavy seas from a destroyer, a daring British boarding party found intact inside the submarine an Enigma machine together with a list of naval cipher keys for every day through June.

The insights acquired enabled the British to read the Hydra cipher throughout the war, long after the pilfered keys were outdated. They also eventually led to the breaking of the Sud and Medusa ciphers, used in the Mediterranean, and the large-ship cipher, Neptun.

During 1942 the Royal Navy could spare scant resources for the Mediterranean, large areas of which were controlled by German aircraft based in Italy and North Africa. Nevertheless, by exploiting enemy ciphers, the British in 1942 sank 230 Italian and 34 German ships in the Mediterranean. The consequent shortages of supplies suffered by the Axis armies in North Africa hastened their demise.

In the Battle of the Atlantic, communications intelligence, or SIGINT, was absolutely decisive. Without a steady infusion of food and munitions across the Atlantic from North America, Great Britain simply could not survive as a nation, nor could the Allies possibly prosecute a war in Europe. During 1942 the Germans came perilously close to choking the Atlantic lifeline.

They had mastered the British and Allied merchant ship cipher, which told them the sailing dates, composition, and routes of convoys. Meanwhile, they shifted their submarines from the Hydra to a new Triton cipher, which initially proved impregnable.

Manned by magnificently skilled and brave crews employing sophisticated wolfpack tactics, the U-boats dispatched Allied merchant ships in horrific numbers — 700,000 tons in June, 730,000 tons in November, more than 6 million tons for the year. Ships were being sunk more rapidly than they could be built, and the U-boat fleet was multiplying ominously.

Late in 1942 Bletchley Park finally broke the new U-boat cipher and soon realized that the Germans were reading the Allies' convoy cipher. Before the Allies could benefit from this breakthrough, the Germans introduced a new version of the Enigma machine and once again made U-boat communications secure. During the first three weeks of March 1943, the Germans sank ninety-five ships in the North Atlantic, and some British strategists began to despair. This could not go on.

Miraculously, in late March Bletchley Park broke back, fathoming the new version of Enigma. Now the Allies knew where the U-boats were. In one of the most dramatic turnabouts of the war, they sank fifty-six U-boats in April and May. During the next three months the Royal Navy sank seventy-four more U-boats, while the Allies lost only fifty-eight ships. The dreaded killers of the North Atlantic now became relentlessly hunted and doomed prey, betrayed by their own words, which Bletchley Park heard and understood.

Early on, the British also broke the cipher employed by German intelligence, the Abwehr, and they caught virtually every German spy who set foot in the United Kingdom, more than 120. Some wound up on the gallows or in prison; others saw fit to serve as carefully controlled double agents. The British endowed them with fictitious subagents and built up illusory spy rings, which developed credibility by forwarding both accurate and inaccurate yet plausible reports. The Abwehr congratulated itself upon the espionage successes and even decorated some of the double and nonexistent agents. The British were able to perpetrate and maintain the hoax because they knew through the cipher what the Abwehr was thinking. Prudently, they conserved this asset for the next critical phase of the war, the invasion of Europe.

The Allies also frequently knew what Hitler and other Nazi leaders were thinking. The Japanese ambassador in Berlin, Baron Oshima, was a meticulous and astute reporter who periodically had long talks with Hitler and his lieutenants as well as with German generals and scientists. When such conversations occurred, the Allies were invisibly present. For Oshima's detailed accounts, transmitted in the Japanese Purple (diplomatic) cipher, were read almost as quickly in London and Washington as in Tokyo. They graphically revealed Hitler's moods, apprehensions, perceptions, and — sometimes — intentions.

The British recognized that Hitler was afflicted by an irrational belief that the Allies eventually would invade Norway and an equally fervent suspicion that they would attack in the Balkans. As the Allies prepared for the Normandy landings, the fictitious German spies in England played on Hitler's predispositions by sending subtle reports contrived to convince him he was right.

Meanwhile the British, largely through the nonexistent spies, created in the minds of the Germans a whole phantom army — the First U.S. Army Group, or FUSAG, notionally comprising eighty-seven divisions allegedly commanded by the ferocious General George S. Patton. The "spies" firmly planted in German thoughts the conviction that the first Allied landings, wherever they occurred, would be a diversion. Once the Germans committed their own forces to deal with the diversionary landing, the mighty FUSAG would make the main strike straight across the English Channel at the Pas de Calais.

When the first of the thirty-five Allied divisions that constituted the invasion force landed at Normandy on June 6, 1944, Hitler had sixteen Wehrmacht divisions in Scandinavia and twenty in the Balkans to defend against the illusory threats. While the Allies secured the beachhead, German commanders kept the entire Fifteenth Wehrmacht uselessly idle at the Pas de Calais waiting for FUSAG. The "spies" kept radioing reports indicating that FUSAG was crouching to leap and assuring that the Normandy landings were a ruse. When the Germans at Normandy identified real American units that had been reported as belonging to FUSAG, they were unfazed. Obviously, the units had been transferred for the diversion. By the time the Germans realized that FUSAG wasn't coming, it was too late.

On August 3, 1944, the British flashed to General Omar Bradley, commander of the Twelfth Army Group at Normandy, one of the single most important decrypts of World War II. It disclosed that Hitler had assumed personal command of the battle and ordered a massive armored attack to seal the twenty-mile Avranches gap through which twelve U.S. divisions had burst out of the beachhead. Notified of precise enemy intentions, Bradley laid down a classic defense, a perfect trap. Betrayed by their ciphers, the Germans marched into it, and there ensued a massacre that cost them nineteen divisions and, soon, all of France.

From 1940 to 1945, deciphered German secrets daily influenced the thought and decisions of British Prime Minister Winston Churchill, who personally read all of the significant intercepts. Broken ciphers kept the British informed of the development and exact capabilities of the German "wonder weapons," the V1 and V2 rockets, the jet aircraft; they enabled the Allies to delay advent of the weapons and to counter them when they appeared. Indeed, the Germans scarcely kept any secrets. At no other time in warfare has one major adversary known as much about another as the Allies knew about the Germans.

Bill Smits and others haunted by the RUS letters understood this history. They understood something else.

British cryptanalysts began with a gift of one German cipher machine. On one occasion they obtained, from *U-110*, keys valid for about eight weeks. Otherwise, they figured everything out for themselves without the assistance of stolen cryptographic materials.

The Americans built a replica of the Japanese cipher machine solely on the basis of theoretical knowledge deduced from analysis of enciphered messages. They never had the benefit of any stolen keys or other materials. Yet they read Japanese ciphers throughout most of the war.

The RUS letters indicated that one or more spies for a protracted if indeterminate period had been giving the Russians technical manuals that diagrammed the logic of American cipher machines as well as keys. If true, then the Soviets had all they needed to decipher secret U.S. communications. If they could do that, they had gained an advantage that was of momentous value in peacetime and potentially fatal in wartime.

As a student of Soviet affairs, Smits found further cause to worry. The Soviet Union was ossified, mired in ever-deepening economic disarray and falling technologically ever farther behind the West. If the Soviets had the decisive advantage the RUS letters implied, then the graying oligarchy — who themselves had not too long to live — might be tempted to exploit it in one last desperate throw of the dice.

3

A Terrible Secret

FOR SIXTEEN YEARS a terrible secret tortured Barbara Walker. Upon discovering it in 1968, she was virtually paralyzed by shame, anger, and conflict. She honestly did not know which came first, her country or her family. And she did not see how she could be faithful to one without betraying the other.

Throughout Barbara Crowley's childhood in Boston, her Catholic parents and mores of the times taught her that she was supposed to marry, bear children, and devote herself to motherhood. In 1957, at age nineteen, she did marry, a sailor who also was nineteen and Catholic. Within six years they had four children, and she was a good mother to them. But once she found out about John Walker, the guilty knowledge poisoned their relationship, and her life began to unravel. More and more she attempted to escape the dilemma through alcohol, which further enfeebled her personally and estranged her from her family.

Still, Barbara Walker never fully capitulated to circumstances or stopped fighting with her conscience. Sometimes she tried to exorcise the curse by drunkenly shouting the secret to her children, who did not comprehend. Twice she telephoned the FBI. Each time, at the critical moment, she indecisively hung up.

After her divorce in 1976, she struggled to keep the family partially intact, taking the two youngest children, Laura, sixteen, and Michael, thirteen, to live with her elderly mother in Skowhegan, Maine. They subsisted on food stamps, welfare payments, and her wages from a shoe factory where she started at $2.65 an hour. As soon as Laura finished high school in 1978, she fled into the army. Michael left in 1980 to join his father, who had retired from the navy and was living in Norfolk, Virginia.

On Memorial Day and the Fourth of July, Barbara would drape an American flag in front of the house and speak to neighbors about her love of country. Sometimes she vowed to herself that ultimately she would do the right thing. But she could not quite bring herself to do it.

In April 1980, after her mother died, Barbara returned to her native Massachusetts and found a job as a store clerk in the resort town of West Dennis. During solitary nights in a tiny apartment above a bookshop, she drank heavily and brooded over the secret, agonizing about what to do. She had no idea how much depended upon what she decided.

In November 1984 she received an unexpected present, a phone call from Laura, who had not spoken to her in more than two years. The same secret that imprisoned the mother afflicted the daughter, and Laura had not fared well since leaving home.

Before her discharge from the army in October 1979, she had entered into an unhappy marriage; and not long after she gave birth to a son, her young husband abandoned her. Later, he absconded with the baby, and she lost track of both. Alone and untrained for any vocation, Laura lived in penury and despondency, eking out an existence from low-paying jobs in Buffalo, New York. She despised her father, pitied her mother, and grieved over her missing child.

Drugs or alcohol might have snared her had it not been for a friend who often watched the Christian Broadcasting Network program "The 700 Club." The program makes counselors available to viewers throughout the country who want help with spiritual or personal problems, and the friend put Laura in contact with one of them. Through the counseling, Laura gradually acquired religious faith and with it a new order and purpose in her life.

In the telephone call, she appealed to her mother to liberate them both from the corrupting secret, to finally do the right thing. "Will you stand by me? Will you support me?" Barbara asked.

"Absolutely."

On Saturday, November 17, 1984, Barbara Walker marshaled all her strength and finally telephoned the FBI field office in Boston to report that John Walker was a spy. Routinely, the Boston office referred the allegation to the small FBI office in Hyannis, Massachusetts, which is near West Dennis.

Were they to confide, some old-time FBI agents would tell you that there is no good reason to maintain an office in Hyannis. Crime and espionage, after all, are not rampant among the wealthy who maintain estates in the area or the retired folk who live in the condominiums there. The veterans suggest that the late J. Edgar Hoover opened a satellite office in Hyannis solely to appease and serve the Kennedys, all of whom he thoroughly loathed.

Be that as it may, chance thrust upon the Hyannis office responsibility for conducting one of the most important interviews in the history of the FBI. The agent sent to talk to Barbara Walker on November 29 — twelve days after her call — had no real training or background in counterintelligence. He was aware that the Thanksgiving and Christmas seasons, like a full moon, tend to bring out the kooks; that a distraught divorcée harboring grievances against a former husband may not be the best of sources. And the condition of Barbara, who gulped vodka during the interview, did not inspire confidence. Nevertheless, the agent listened politely (FBI agents from their first day in the bureau are conditioned to be courteous to all; they even shoot criminals courteously).

In a rambling and discursive account, Barbara averred that Walker while in the navy had been a Soviet spy and received large sums of money for espionage. On two occasions years ago she had driven with him into the Virginia countryside south of Washington and waited in the car while he slipped into the woods carrying a sack containing film hidden beneath trash. An hour or so later he stopped the car a couple of miles away and again went into the woods. He returned with thirty-five thousand dollars in cash. She suspected that her former husband, who now ran his own private detective agency in Norfolk, was in some way still involved in espionage. Just a few years ago he had tried to persuade their daughter Laura to sell him army secrets.

Although the agent dutifully took notes and asked a few perfunctory questions, he did not press for amplification or evidence in support of this tale. To him, talk of a spy ring, of father recruiting daughter, seemed far-fetched and the intoxicated source unreliable. So he thanked Barbara and bade her good-day.

At least the agent eventually wrote a report that faithfully reflected what Barbara had said. However, he designated it "65–0." The 65 indicated that the subject of the report was espionage; the o signified that the information it contained merited no investigation or action.

When the report arrived in the Boston office of the FBI, an agent or clerk should have examined the contents before deciding on its disposition. Probably, though, the reviewer that day had to sort through hundreds of reports and thus merely glanced at the numerical designation. However it happened, the report wound up in the Zero File, a repository for records that are to be filed and forgotten. Hence, the FBI did nothing about the specific allegations that a Soviet spy was at large in Virginia.

Mystified by the inaction, Laura Walker on January 24, 1985, called the FBI in Boston and asked what it intended to do about her traitorous father. Her inquiry did not elicit a clear response, nor did it stimulate any action.

Every three months in FBI field offices a supervisor must inspect the Zero File. It is dreary duty because virtually all reports labeled with a zero are worth just that, nothing. Nevertheless, headquarters insists upon a quarterly review as a bureaucratic back-up, a safety check to ensure that nothing important slips through the cracks.

In February a Boston supervisor making the mandatory quarterly check picked up the report of Barbara Walker's allegations and recognized that a deplorable mistake had been made in ignoring them. Hurriedly, he drafted an AIRTEL (confidential overnight letter) summarizing the report and dispatched it to headquarters, omitting the damning date of the interview with Barbara. Recriminations, if called for, could come later; it was more important now to rectify the lapse of many weeks.

FBI records today do not reveal who opened the AIRTEL in Washington the next morning. They do show that whoever received the intelligence buried it, either in the files or a desk, without consulting anybody or taking any action whatsoever. The United States had had three chances to act upon Barbara Walker's revelations and muffed them all.

It was to have yet a fourth opportunity. The Boston supervisor prudently sent a copy of the AIRTEL to the field office in Norfolk because John Walker resided there. There, every-thing depended upon one man, Joseph R. Wolfinger.

Sandy-haired, with a ruddy complexion, and granny glasses frequently perched on the end of his nose, Wolfinger in a frayed Brooks Brothers shirt open at the collar reminded one of a harried country lawyer. He reinforced the image by speaking in a rich Southern drawl and affecting the homely mannerisms of a good old boy who could belt down bourbon with the best of them while saluting the stately portrait of Robert E. Lee above his fireplace.

Those who knew him paid no attention to the pose. The son of a patrician and moneyed Southern family, Wolfinger had grown up in cultured comfort, read extensively, and traveled widely. After graduation from the University of South Carolina Law School, he joined the FBI out of patriotism and a sense of noblesse oblige, intending after a few years to establish a gentlemanly law practice of his own.

The challenges of the FBI engrossed him, he believed the work worthwhile for the country, and he never got around to leaving. The bureau in 1977 assigned him to its embryonic counterintelligence Analytical Unit at headquarters. Then it chose him to oversee the installation and introduction of a huge computer system for counterintelligence use throughout the country. His management of the complex project gained him plaudits, a promotion, and tacit acceptance into the head-quarters hierarchy. But Wolfinger wanted to run operations, not computers, and he kept requesting a transfer back to the field, even at the price of a reduction in grade. Superiors par-ried the requests because the computer system was function-ing so productively they did not want to tinker with it by let-ting him go. He had become a prisoner of his own success.

Finally, in late 1983, somebody decided that Wolfinger deserved the reward he desired, and the FBI put him in charge of operations in his hometown, Norfolk. Thus it happened that on the same misty February morning that the AIRTEL was shelved in Washington, Joe Wolfinger opened a copy in Norfolk.

Just as Janet Fournier, John Peterson, and Bill Smits in San Francisco from the first believed that the RUS letters were authentic, Wolfinger from the first believed Barbara Walker. To someone who understood the techniques of Soviet espionage, her account of the expedition into the northern Virginia woods was an account of the depositing of secrets at a drop and the recovery of cash and probably instructions from another drop site. She, a housewife, accurately described basic and classic Soviet tradecraft. There was another element of plausibility. If, as she said, her husband was a communications specialist, then he would be a target of supreme interest to the Soviets. Barbara claimed that her former husband attempted to lure their daughter into espionage. If she was fabricating, she scarcely would volunteer such information, which made part of her story readily susceptible to checking. In Wolfinger's judgment, her story cried out for investigation, and obviously an investigation should begin with an interrogation of the daughter.

Laura, though, lived in Buffalo, far beyond his domain, and only headquarters could order an interview with her. If the case proved to be of the magnitude Wolfinger suspected it might, he would require much more help from headquarters. Navy cooperation would have to be enlisted; interviews elsewhere in the country might be needed as well as special authority to conduct surveillances.

Within the hour, Wolfinger telephoned David Szady in Washington and asked him if he recently had read any interesting mail from Boston. Szady had not.

"Well, I've come across something I think has a great deal

46

of potential," Wolfinger said. "I'm going to need a lot of support. Right now, I need authorization to begin a full investigation."

"You've got it."

"Thanks. I'll explain in a memo."

Technically, Wolfinger was justified in calling Szady, who from headquarters coordinated FBI operations against Soviet military intelligence, known as the GRU. Of course, even assuming that John Walker was or had been a spy, Wolfinger had no evidence to indicate whether he belonged to the GRU or much larger KGB. The more important a case, the greater the likelihood that it is being handled by the KGB, the dominant Soviet service. But if pressed, Wolfinger could argue that he assumed Walker was GRU property because it specializes in collecting intelligence about the U.S. military. Nobody could gainsay him because nobody knew anything.

Actually, Wolfinger did not care. In calling Szady, he was engaging in what FBI agents call shopping, an irregular, unsanctioned solicitation of a patron who will authorize an agent to do what must be done and conspire with him in doing it. Wolfinger turned to Szady both because he understood his mentality and because they were personal friends, though in some ways the two men scarcely could have been more different.

Szady stood just over six feet four inches tall and weighed a lean 170 pounds, about the same as in high school. He also retained much of the physical strength, quickness, and agility of the basketball player he had been. His coal-black hair, equally dark eyes, thick eyebrows, and hawkish face, together with a rangy bearing, gave him the look of a man at home in rough streets and bars. He had seen many of both.

David Szady came from the mill town of Holyoke, Massachusetts, whose congested tenements were peopled with Irish, Polish, and French Catholics, most of whom were immigrants or first-generation Americans. His father dropped out of high school after one year and went to work in a factory; his mother toiled in a paper mill; his grandfather ran numbers for petty gamblers. They lived on the upper floor of a two-story frame duplex in the Polish section, and on occasion as many as fifteen relatives stayed with them for days at a time.

Each workday the father rose at 5:00 A.M. to walk to work at a compressor factory and came home at 4:30 P.M. for supper, always served promptly upon his arrival. He never earned more than seven thousand dollars a year, and some years, because of layoffs, he made considerably less. When Szady was thirteen, his father took him to the plant and showed him the machine at which he worked. Szady recoiled from the heat and pounding noise it emitted. "This is how I spend my life," his father said. "This is not how I want you to spend yours. You must get an education. In this country, with an education and hard work, you can do anything. You can even be a doctor."

From age fourteen on, Szady did work hard, after school and in the summer. He delivered flowers, swept library floors, and as a chipper cleaned filthy oil and garbage from the machinery at his father's plant. Another summer he labored as a hopper in a textile mill, gulping salt pills in 120-degree heat, crawling on hands and knees to roll heavy fabrics into huge trucks bound for New York. A third summer he toiled as a shipper in a paper mill alongside blacks and Puerto Ricans who spoke in curdling obscenities.

They accepted him as one of them. "The Captain," a 325-pound numbers king and potentate at the paper mill, used to invite Szady to his ghetto home in nearby Springfield on Saturday nights. With the Captain and his friends, Szady drank cheap gin, traded ribald tales, ate fried chicken, fried fish, corn bread, and green beans cooked with ham hock, and learned of another world. He also learned in the bars, which together with the churches were the social centers of Holyoke. He saw drunk husbands slink homeward evading wives ringing Salvation Army bells and collecting for church charities on the street. He saw almost everybody gamble, though nobody could afford it. To him, though, the workers of all ethnic backgrounds were largely good, generous, and industrious people sustained by strong family ties and traditions. Most shared his father's belief in work and his dream that their children through education would elevate themselves to a better life. He never found cause to be ashamed of having been one of them.

By hard work, Szady put himself through two small New England colleges, obtaining a liberal arts degree and a master's degree in chemistry. While supporting a wife and two small children by teaching and coaching basketball, he earned a master's degree in education from the University of New Hampshire and seemed destined to be a teacher for life.

Late in 1972, when Szady was twenty-eight, a police officer with whom he attended church mentioned that the FBI was increasing the number of its agents and suggested that he think about a career with the bureau. The prospect intrigued him. In Holyoke the FBI was perhaps the most respected of all American institutions outside the church. His parents would be almost as proud of an FBI agent as they would be of a doctor.

Then as now, the FBI accepted only about one of every one hundred agent applicants. During a heavy snowfall in Boston, Szady underwent searching interrogation by three inquisitors who undertook to gauge his character, bearing, courage, and ability to deal with people. The written examinations tried to measure native intelligence, general knowledge, and capacity to think quickly under stress. One essay question asked, "Why did the Articles of Confederation fail?" Thankfully recalling a tenth-grade history teacher, Szady accurately wrote: "They did not create a central government strong enough to unite and govern the colonies as a nation." The last examination was a spelling quiz, and Szady stumbled over the word *xenophobia*. A heretofore aloof FBI agent remarked, "Don't worry. In the bureau we have dictionaries." Szady sensed he had made it, and he had.

Fortunately for him, the examinations did not include questions about geography. Toward the end of his basic training in Quantico, Virginia, he telephoned his wife in New England. "We're going to Alabama."

"Where is Alabama?"

"I don't know. I always thought it was a football team. I didn't know it was a place. Get a map and look for a town called Mobile."

As a rookie agent in a small and relatively tranquil Southern city, Szady had no opportunity to perform spectacular feats of investigation. He did induce a number of people, particularly blacks who often were suspicious of white law enforcement officers, to assist the FBI. This ability caught the attention of superiors and may have influenced the FBI decision in 1974 to post him to the Washington field office, a traditional training ground for future FBI leaders.

In Washington Szady soon joined a squad deployed against the KGB and for the next seven years participated in virtually all phases of counterintelligence — undercover guises, surveillance, recruitment, double agent operations, and agent handling. Along the way, he acquired a patina that enabled him to navigate in high as well as low social and professional climes. He took up golf as much for social as recreational purposes. Presiding over a meeting, he could say, "Gentlemen, today we want to identify, isolate, and, I would hope, liquidate the problem."

He also could and sometimes did say, "Come to the fucking

point and let's get on with it!" Some thought him too straightforward, too blunt; that he bulldozed too heedlessly to the point. But, as headquarters noted, Szady's cases more often than not came out well, and strong people gravitated to him.

At forty-one, Szady was proud of his family, his home in the Virginia suburbs, and his career. He was especially proud of his oldest son, who was both a star football player and such a brilliant math student that as a high school junior he already was contributing to research for the National Aeronautics and Space Administration. Prestigious universities in Virginia and California were courting him with offers of scholarships. But he set his heart on a program at Princeton University, which welcomed him but offered no scholarship. On a Saturday afternoon in the backyard, Szady and his wife had decided it. They would take a second mortgage on the house, and she would find a job. The boy would go to Princeton no matter what the cost (roughly eighty thousand dollars for four undergraduate years).

One of Szady's neighbors in northern Virginia was Joe Wolfinger. Just as the Captain had prepared Szady to relate to blacks in Alabama, Mobile gentry had equipped him to understand Wolfinger. The two rode in the same car-pool, their families dined together and cared for each other's children when parents were away. Wolfinger came to recognize in Szady a kindred spirit, an unregenerate field man who believed that the ultimate function of headquarters with respect to agents running live operations was to get them what they needed rather than to get in their way.

When Wolfinger telephoned requesting authorization to investigate John Walker, he was confident of the answer he would receive. He also knew that in accordance with FBI procedures, the instant Szady issued the authorization, he would become the headquarters supervisor thereafter responsible for the whole John Walker case.

Pursuant to a request from Szady, two FBI agents late in the afternoon of March 7, 1985, visited Laura Walker at her one-room apartment in Buffalo. A pretty brunette with soft, dark eyes and a flawless complexion, she welcomed them calmly and seemed completely composed. The agents primarily wanted her to answer one question: Had her father ever asked her to sell secret military information? Laura forthrightly said yes; he had done so many times. She explained.

As a child, Laura sensed the existence of a malign "family secret," the nature of which she then did not know. She remembered that the family had been very poor, then suddenly had plenty of money. She also recalled that her father kept his den locked and forbade the children ever to enter it.

While Laura was in the army and stationed at Fort Gordon, Georgia, John Walker unexpectedly visited her. His appearance surprised and delighted her because for years he had displayed no interest in her. He questioned her closely about her duties in communications, the equipment she was being trained to operate, and about ciphers. But that was all.

Late in the summer of 1979 Laura, recently married and pregnant, traveled to Norfolk on leave, and her father summoned her to talk about "something important." He asked if she would like to earn a lot of money even at the risk of spending a couple of years in prison. The army, he argued, was tantamount to prison, so she had nothing to lose and might as well exploit the military to make money. He urged her to have an abortion so she could remain in the army, be a good soldier, and wriggle her way into a position affording access to ciphers and other communications secrets. When Laura declined to commit herself, he handed her a hundred dollars and said, "This is only the beginning."

After she returned to duty at Fort Polk, Louisiana, Walker telephoned several times importuning her "to work" for him. In September he flew to Louisiana and appealed to her anew to accept his "offer." Laura almost acquiesced simply because she craved her father's affection, attention, and approval. With difficulty, she finally said no, and the next month she left the army because of pregnancy.

For more than two years, Laura heard nothing more from Walker. Then in February 1982, while she was living in Hayward, California, he again appeared unexpectedly. He led her into a park. "My offer still stands," he announced. If Laura would reenlist in the military, photograph secret documents and cipher material and give them to him, her fortune would be assured. She would receive a retainer of five hundred dollars a month plus substantial payments for each delivery of classified data. The more valuable the secrets stolen, the higher the payments would be. However, Walker said, his "man in Europe" worried that soon she would be too old to reenlist. Therefore, she must act now. She refused.

Not long afterward, Walker mailed her five hundred dollars, "a token of good will" from his "man in Europe." Laura did not respond, and thereafter her father ignored her.

As Laura completed her narrative, the two agents momentarily masked their emotions with silence. Then one gently asked if Laura would sign a written statement embodying all she had related. She nodded affirmatively.

Might they talk to her again tomorrow? Yes, she was resolved to cooperate in any way she could.

To the Buffalo agents, and to Wolfinger and Szady, who studied their reports, Laura appeared to be a credible and competent witness. By providing sinister corroboration of her mother's allegations, her testimony made clear that the FBI should listen carefully to Barbara Walker.

At Szady's behest, the Boston office dispatched two agents to question Barbara Walker comprehensively. The interrogation began March 19 at her apartment in West Dennis. Although Barbara of her own initiative acknowledged that she was an alcoholic, she spoke soberly, rationally, and in appalling detail about events that convinced her John Walker was a Soviet spy.

She first became suspicious in 1968, when he was stationed at COMSUBLANT (Commander, Submarines, Atlantic), a navy command in Norfolk. A small café he owned in South Carolina had failed, leaving the family in acute financial straits. Mysteriously, their financial problems evaporated almost overnight. Although his navy pay remained the same, Walker suddenly had sufficient cash to move the family into an expensive apartment and buy more than five thousand dollars' worth of new furniture and two sailboats, one costing fifty-five hundred dollars.

Acting on her suspicions, Barbara one afternoon searched her husband's desk and found a Minox camera and a metal box. Inside the box were rolls of film; a hand-drawn map; photographs of roads, trees, and bushes, with arrows pointing to specific locations; and a note saying, "Information not what we wanted, want information on rotor." (At the time, rotors controlled some American cipher machines.)

Glancing up, Barbara saw Walker staring at her from the doorway, his face fixed with rage. Advancing menacingly, he shouted, "Get out of there!"

"Traitor! Traitor!" she screamed.

He slapped her hard and yelled, "Shut up!"

During the ensuing days, months, and years, Walker neither denied nor apologized for spying. Sometimes he even talked to Barbara about it, albeit cautiously and elliptically. Once he intimated that he had contracted to supply "them" with navy secrets so long as he stayed in the service. Both understood that "them" meant the Soviets. To her moral protests and censure, he retorted, "You'd be surprised how many are doing it." He dismissed her occasional threats to expose him as the empty posturing of a drunk who would never dare bring down ruin on her family.

Barbara recounted more specifically than she had the previous November her ventures with Walker into the countryside of Fairfax County, Virginia. She recalled that in 1969 after Walker picked up thirty-five thousand dollars in fifty- and hundred-dollar bills, he made her tape part of the cash to her body before they flew from Washington to California, where he then was stationed.

As further evidence of lavish Soviet payments to Walker, she cited other major purchases he had made while his only ostensible income was from the navy: a Cessna airplane; a houseboat; building lots in Nassau; lots in Tampa and St. Petersburg, Florida; and two waterfront lots in Kitty Hawk, North Carolina. Additionally, Walker treated the children to dinners at fine restaurants, costly vacations, and expensive clothes.

There was more. Not only was John Walker a spy; his brother Arthur, a retired navy lieutenant commander, also was a spy. Barbara believed John recruited him. In any case, Arthur certainly knew about Walker's spying because he and Barbara discussed it.

Their son, Michael, a seaman aboard the aircraft carrier *Nimitz,* also knew of his father's involvement in espionage. He had pleaded with Barbara not to betray Walker on grounds that exposure would ruin his naval career. Michael, however, had never mentioned any espionage entreaties from his father, and she was sure the boy was not implicated.

Although not certain, she suspected that Walker still was engaged in espionage, possibly in collusion with a navy chief petty officer named Wentworth who, she thought, was somewhere in California.

One of the agents asked Barbara if she would voluntarily

undergo a polygraph examination. "I will take it anytime you say," she replied. At last, Barbara Walker had liberated herself.

The FBI evaluated her statements to the Boston agents as sincere, convincing, and appalling in their implications. Yet her testimony, even though buttressed by that of Laura, fell far short of legal proof. And it left unanswered the most critical operational question: Assuming John Walker was a Soviet spy while in the navy, was he still an active spy who threatened the United States? Barbara suspected that he was; however, she had no firsthand knowledge of any clandestine activities by him subsequent to their divorce in 1976. His overtures to Laura in 1982 suggested that as of then he still was trying to steal classified information. That was 1982; what about 1985? Perhaps, Szady thought, Laura could help.

Like her mother, Laura had committed herself to a moral course and was determined to follow it. She also liked FBI agent Paul Culligan, who treated her respectfully and in his honesty manifested the personal rectitude absent in her father. So early on, she volunteered to cooperate in the investigation however she could.

Coached by the FBI, Laura telephoned Walker in Norfolk, and with her signed consent, the FBI recorded the conversation. As any daughter might, she reported her circumstances and listed several fictitious job possibilities contrived to interest a spy. There was an opening in the army reserves, where she could take advantage of her communications training. Eastman Kodak, which, as the Soviets know, is a world leader in optics, might have a secretarial position for her. The Central Intelligence Agency had given her a preemployment examination, but she hesitated to apply because of fear that "in certain areas" she might fail a CIA lie detector test.

Szady received the transcript of the fifty-five-minute conversation in early April. It showed Walker reacting warily to the call from a daughter with whom he had had no contact for almost three years. Nevertheless, to Szady, Walker gave himself away, first by interjecting that Laura's fear of the polygraph was "a legitimate concern." Later he angrily complained that the summer before, during a brief encounter in Norfolk, Barbara threatened to reveal "certain knowledge."

"Legitimate concern" and "certain knowledge" about what, if not espionage? By these remarks alone, Walker confirmed that he, his wife, and his daughter owned the same secret, that the essence of the allegations against him was accurate. Although none of Walker's guarded words specifically demonstrated that he still was spying, they clearly beckoned Laura to join him in an ongoing conspiracy. He was concerned about present as well as past enterprises.

Szady calculated. If Walker remained in espionage, as his conversation with Laura suggested, that meant he had hidden confederates. After retiring from the navy in 1976, he himself had no access to classified information. He could only depend on others who did.

Barbara named the brother, Arthur Walker. The FBI already knew he had been out of the navy for twelve years, even longer than John. In his current job as a low-level employee in a consulting firm concerned with ship repairs, he appeared to have modest access to secrets. Barbara and Laura as well referred to another navy man, "Jerry Wentworth." But the FBI had been unable to find traces of anybody named Wentworth who approximated their descriptions.

It was vital to ascertain all Walker had done; it was more vital, by watching him, to identify whoever was stealing secrets for him to deliver to the Soviets. That person — or those persons — constituted the greater danger.

By law, the FBI may not tap a telephone, emplace listening devices, or employ other intrusive investigative techniques against a citizen suspected of espionage without express approval of the Foreign Intelligence Surveillance Court. To obtain authorization, it must persuade a judge of the court that there is probable cause to believe that the target of the surveillance is acting for a foreign power. Before approaching a judge, agents first must convince the Justice Department that their evidence is authentic and compelling.

That Saturday afternoon, Justice Department attorneys who came in blue jeans to confer with Szady at FBI headquarters agreed that the collective statements of Barbara and Laura Walker, together with the telephone transcript, composed sufficient evidence. They agreed, too, that the FBI should seek surveillance authorization immediately.

In the late afternoon, Szady called on a federal judge in the Watergate Apartments on the bank of the Potomac near Georgetown. While the judge read the FBI submission in his study, Szady stepped onto a balcony to afford him privacy. In the spring twilight he could see the graves of Arlington Cemetery across the river, the mansion of Robert E. Lee, and the tiny flame that flickers continuously above the tomb of John F. Kennedy. Below, the streets of Foggy Bottom lined with trees freshly green were placid and pretty. He thought of other streets and Saturday nights in Massachusetts and wondered what the Captain was doing.

Sometimes judges ask for more information or explanations. Not that night. "You have the authorization herewith," said the judge. "As a citizen, I hope you exercise it immediately." Szady apologized for intruding. "No, I understand. Good luck." From a phone booth Szady cryptically informed Wolfinger of the clearance.

To lead the investigation in Norfolk, Wolfinger picked Robert W. Hunter, a soft-spoken, bespectacled agent of medium height and build whom few would have taken for a tenacious investigator. In 1983 he tracked down and arrested a sailor attempting to sell the Russians lists of targets in the Soviet Union the navy would eradicate if the United States were attacked. Friends said he so immersed himself in the case that he impaired his health and marriage, which now was ending sadly in divorce. Most of the other Norfolk agents were young, and several were on their first FBI assignment. Soon Wolfinger would impress them all into the investigation and virtually suspend all other operations.

One dominant rule governed the investigation: Agents must refrain from any action likely to alert Walker. If during surveillance they had to choose between losing him and being detected by him, they were to let him go. Inquiries outside government agencies had to be sufficiently subtle to conceal the fact that Walker was the object of them. Only if Walker was kept ignorant of the investigation could he be expected to lead the FBI to his presumed American collaborators and Soviet controllers.

Just as the FBI was about to tap Walker's telephone and begin the surveillance, Barbara Walker bravely contributed to keeping him in ignorance. She came to Norfolk to visit her daughter Margaret in early April, and Wolfinger assigned Hunter and a bright female agent, Beverly Andress, to watch over her. A slender woman in her late twenties with flowing brown hair, Andress was the wife of an FBI agent based in Washington. Men in the office regarded her as both a "classy lady" and a poised colleague whom they would trust alongside them on any mission. She quickly established a feminine rapport with Barbara and persuaded her that it was supremely important to keep Walker ignorant of the investigation.

Learning that Barbara was with their daughter, Walker telephoned the night of April 10 and demanded to see her. "I know what you want to talk about," she said. "You don't have

to worry. I haven't done it. I don't have the nerve to do it."
Nevertheless, Walker insisted upon a face-to-face talk, and
though afraid, Barbara agreed to see him the next evening.

He took her to a McDonald's for dinner and like a master
espionage case officer endeavored simultaneously to domi-
nate and entice her. "You know, you killed the goose that laid
the golden egg," he said. "If I hadn't had to leave the navy
because of your threats, I could have made a million dollars
more."

Walker stated that the several "operatives" who worked for
him while he was in the navy also had left the service and that
he now had no money. He did have promising prospects of
developing land in South Carolina, and Barbara could expect
to benefit from the profits.

"I've talked to all the children except Margaret," Walker
said. "They all agree that you must not say anything. If you
do, you would ruin Michael's career."

Barbara's heart pounded with fear. "Are you saying Michael's working for you?"

"No, no. I'm not saying that. It's just that he's up for secret
clearance, and if you said anything, it would ruin him."

Implicit in all Walker said that evening was a conviction that
she had not reported him.

As Barbara recounted the conversation to agents Hunter
and Andress, they admired her courage. She had been very
afraid to meet Walker; afraid of physical abuse; afraid she
might not be strong enough to hide her cooperation with the
FBI. But she had overcome her fear and, as she in years past
vowed, she had done "the right thing" for her country. She
looked better and displayed vestiges of the handsome woman
she had been — tall, with fine facial bone structure, large dark
eyes, lustrous black hair. Maybe she looked better because
now she was anticipating a new freedom, freedom from alco-

hol. She had resolved to enter a hospital for treatment on her return to Massachusetts.

While reassured that Walker seemingly did not suspect that he was under investigation, the FBI was perplexed by his statements implying he no longer was "in the business." The preponderance of opinion was that the insinuations represented an effort to mollify and disarm Barbara. Yet they raised an element of doubt.

The necessity not to alert Walker imposed considerable limitations on the investigators. But within the limits, they scoured Walker's background. As details accumulated, Wolfinger, Szady, and the headquarters Analytical Unit began to see two quite different John Walkers.

There was John A. Walker, Jr., the successful serviceman and responsible citizen. A high school dropout who enlisted in the navy at age seventeen, Walker by his own merits had risen from seaman to chief warrant officer, a rank that gave him most of the perquisites of a commissioned officer. He performed well in demanding communications billets aboard ships, nuclear submarines, and at Atlantic Fleet headquarters. The navy reposed such confidence in him that for many years it trusted him to process the most secret documents and cryptographic data.

In a 1972 fitness report a commanding officer evaluated Walker as follows:

> CWO-2 Walker is intensely loyal, taking great pride in himself and the naval service, fiercely supporting its principles and traditions. He possesses a fine sense of personal honor and integrity, coupled with a great sense of humor. He is friendly, intelligent and possesses the ability to work in close harmony with others. He is especially at ease in social situations and has an active self-improvement program which includes enrollment in the commercial instrument flying course and the completion

of the naval intelligence correspondence course. He is an active sailboat enthusiast and an accomplished aircraft pilot (private license). CWO-2 Walker's division sponsors a Little League baseball team which finished first in the league.

Another fitness report said of Walker:

> He conducted a course in sailing for Boy Scouts, and his division sponsors a Little League baseball team. CWO-2 Walker pursues a vigorous self-improvement program which now includes aircraft instrument ground school, Spanish and a naval intelligence correspondence course. Mr. Walker's outstanding supervision of his staff composed of E5–E8 petty officers has resulted in an effective division with very high morale, great esprit de corps and the professional reputation of being the very heart of communications training. Mr. Walker's impeccable personal and military appearance, demeanor, fine sense of humor and social grace and demonstrated performance indicate his outstanding potential for positions of greater responsibility.

Later, in civilian life, Walker became known as an excellent and reliable private investigator who gave clients good value for their money. Local police and corporate customers regarded him highly. He was an active member of the Better Business Bureau and served without compensation on its Consumer Arbitration Board. A Norfolk television station singled him out for praise because of his public-spirited efforts to locate missing children.

Bald, five feet nine inches tall, and slightly overweight at 170 pounds, Walker was not physically prepossessing. When he donned an expensive hairpiece, though, he acquired a kind of raffish, debonair countenance, and his quick mind, flamboyance, and humor attracted desirable women. Among his girlfriends were a former model, a pretty policewoman, and a lovely young black woman. Acquaintances considered him politically conservative and an outspoken anticommunist, a rather unpredictable practical joker but altogether a very solid citizen.

The other John Walker the FBI saw was a satanic figure bereft of any values or principles, a demonic Svengali who pitilessly dominated and exploited men, women, and children for his own corrupt purposes.

As a teenager, he committed four serious burglaries and joined the navy only to escape punishment. He habitually referred to the devoted wife who had borne him four children in less than six years as "Bitch Breath," to the children themselves as "the little bastards," and to his in-laws as "the assholes in Maine." When failure of a business venture mired him in debt, he tried to force his wife into prostitution to improve the family finances. After she found out about his spying, he psychologically and legally made her a coconspirator by taking her on clandestine missions, compelling her to transport Soviet money, and giving her funds the illicit source of which she knew.

He bribed his own brother. He argued for the abortion of his own grandchild in the hope that his daughter would betray the United States for his profit. He did not shrink from the possibility of sending his own daughter to prison.

There was also another side to John Walker the private detective. A pending lawsuit accused him of illegally invading the property of a woman by posing variously as a "Boy Scout leader looking for a campsite, a surveyor purporting to survey the land, a birdwatcher attempting to take pictures of wildlife and a Catholic priest."

Walker additionally hunted fugitives for bounty and kidnapped people. In a personal message he described one abduction:

We have been busier than shit in the office. We just finished
an eight-day executive protection detail in which we assisted a
family in grabbing a kid who was in a cult. The cult is called
the Quest, whatever the shit that means. This kid is about 24
and was under the mind control of this cult and was turning his
paycheck over to 'em. And left his wife. Really a fucked-up
creep. We helped the family grab him. And we took him out to
a cottage in Sandbridge and guarded him and the family and the
deprogrammer, who tries to unbrainwash these kids. What an
operation! We rented a van and snatched that little shit and
threw him in the back, rode off with three cars. It was something else, man. You should have seen it.

Beyond what records and third parties disclosed about
Walker, the agents who listened to his telephone conversations and followed him saw for themselves that he was a formidable antagonist. Throughout April and the first weeks of
May, his words and deeds yielded not a single clue about what
the FBI desperately wanted to know. Was the supposition that
Walker remained a spy erroneous? If not, then who were his
sources? How did he communicate with the Soviets? And
who and where was Wentworth?

4

Unmasking RUS

THROUGH THE AUTUMN of 1984 and winter of 1985, Bill Smits and John Peterson recurrently brooded about RUS. In their minds, the specter of the live espionage network he represented overshadowed all other cases. They taxed themselves personally for not doing more to hunt him down, for not being inventive enough to lure him out of hiding. They even went so far as to propose that the government consider granting some form of immunity.

The proposal was a bureaucratic ball-buster because it presented a dilemma demanding fine and unavoidably controversial judgments. There were many valid arguments — operational, legal, moral, political, and practical — against awarding immunity and anonymity to any traitor. The FBI, after all, is in business to catch spies, not coddle them. Given the horrific implications of the RUS letters, however, Smits and Peterson wondered whether in his case an exception might not be justified. The decision entailed national consequences and was beyond their competence to make, but they hoped that higher authorities would consider the matter and decide.

In Washington, it was much easier to ignore than to confront the issue, and that is what happened. Headquarters did not even acknowledge their letter.*

When Smits and Peterson had to work late, they sometimes dined at the Phnom Penh, a tiny, inexpensive restaurant on the corner of Larkin Street and an alley near the FBI offices. Owned and staffed by refugees from the genocide in Cambodia, the Phnom Penh serves dishes native to that once lovely land. Among them are light spring rolls with a piquant carrot sauce; a salad of shredded green papaya, diced pork, and prawns in lemon dressing; a soup of chicken cubes and pineapple in spicy red curry, coconut milk, and tamarind sauce; catfish fried in a kind of marinade; winter melon and tomato stuffed with chopped pork and prawns in a light brown sauce; sautéed calamari with bamboo shoots. Although Peterson rated the food equal to any Oriental cuisine available in San Francisco, the restaurant generally is uncrowded in the evening because people tend to avoid the neighborhood after dark.

Of the ten small tables, the one by the front bay window provides relative privacy and security. One night in mid-March 1985 Smits and Peterson sat there. The exact date has been forgotten, but it was before the first reports about John Walker reached San Francisco. Relishing the spring rolls, Smits remarked, "I wonder what James Durward Harper is having for supper tonight."

It was his way of bringing up the case of a California businessman imprisoned for life on espionage charges — a case

---

*In August 1984 the FBI learned that one of its own agents, Richard W. Miller, was engaged in an illicit relationship with a suspected Soviet spy. The FBI rushed Donald Stukey, director of Soviet counterintelligence, and some of his leading lieutenants from headquarters to Los Angeles to supervise the investigation of Miller. They remained in California, wholly preoccupied with the Miller case, for more than a year. Thus, during critical stages of the Walker case, FBI headquarters was denuded of key counterintelligence leaders.
Miller was convicted of espionage and sentenced to life in prison in 1986.

Smits initiated in 1982. After the FBI arrested James Durward Harper, he confessed to selling the Poles (and thereby the Soviets) very secret technical data purloined by his wife from a Silicon Valley firm where she was a secretary. Press accounts stated that the data related to future U.S. plans to protect American missiles from surprise attack. Such accounts were accurate but not all that informative. Actually, Harper sold the Poles the basic conceptual technology for what has become known as the Strategic Defense Initiative, or Star Wars. Through Harper, the Soviets long ago saw just how effective SDI might be in neutralizing their missiles. This foreknowledge may explain their desperate ongoing efforts to prevent the United States from developing the system.

Smits habitually reassessed old cases in hope of gleaning insights about new ones, and he believed there was a parallel between Harper and RUS. Through a reputable attorney, Harper had attempted anonymously to negotiate with the FBI for immunity in return for information. During the process, the FBI identified and arrested him without forfeiting the right to prosecute. Smits repeated to Peterson his conviction that subsequent newspaper publicity about the negotiations, which omitted their results, inspired RUS to write the first letter asking for immunity. "Some way, we must do with RUS what we did with Harper," he said.

"We tried."

"Well, we have to try again. We can't just sit around wallowing in Weltschmerz and doing nothing."

"What are we wallowing in?"

"Weltschmerz. It's hard to translate exactly. It means sorrow or worry about the whole world or, more loosely, about something you can't do anything about."

Peterson mumbled, "Sure, Count."

The waiter, who was about four feet tall, asked if they cared for tea. Smits ordered a Coca-Cola. Following the Khmer custom of formally addressing people by the first name, the waiter said to Peterson, "You, Mr. John?"

"Tea, please."

"You know that kid?" Smits asked after the waiter turned away.

"I talk to him. He speaks a little Vietnamese. He's no kid; he's twenty-seven. Malnutrition stunted his growth after they threw everybody out of the cities in Cambodia. But he's lucky. He got through the jungles into Vietnam and joined the boat people. They started out in a rowboat. Didn't know where the hell they were going. The ocean or pirates got most of them. A Japanese freighter picked him up. He's been here about two years. Works his ass off learning the restaurant business and English. Dreams about finding a girl. He's afraid he's too short. Lost his whole family in the jungles."

Suddenly, Peterson was back with the marines in Indochina. As he talked about the communist slaughter of millions of Cambodians after Vietnam fell, anger fueled anger, and he began to curse.

Smits quietly interrupted. "You're attracting attention."

Peterson quickly composed himself. "Sorry. Cambodia has nothing to do with RUS."

As much to himself as to Peterson, Smits said, "It just might."

"What do you mean?"

"Oh, nothing, probably nothing," Smits replied, rousing himself from his thoughts. "About RUS. Let's advertise again. There's nothing to lose. If you think of anything else, let me know."

Outside, Smits wished he had taken along a sweater. The night had turned cold, and lashing winds whipped up swirls of dust and trash on the street. They heard the little waiter calling, "Mr. John." Holding out a twenty-dollar bill, he said, "You forgot money."

68

"It's for you."

The waiter smiled and pressed the money into Peterson's hand. "Too much. You come back soon."

In the morning, Peterson drafted a message and scheduled its publication in the *Los Angeles Times* on three successive Mondays, April 1, 8, and 15. It said, "Rus: Haven't heard from you in some time. Request current status. Still think a deal can be struck to benefit both of us. We are concerned; waiting to hear from you."

While they waited daily in hope of some reaction from RUS, Szady sent Smits summaries of the initial interviews with Barbara and Laura Walker. He accompanied them with a request that the San Francisco office locate and discreetly investigate a Jerry Wentworth in San Leandro, California.

One summary stated: "Mrs. WALKER believes that JOHN recruited his brother, ARTHUR WALKER, a retired lieutenant commander in the UNITED STATES NAVY, and a friend, JERRY WENTWORTH, an active-duty UNITED STATES NAVY communications specialist, into his espionage activities from 1968 to 1976."

Another said, "LAURA advised she believes her father, JOHN ANTHONY WALKER, is still involved in the illegal sale of classified United States information inasmuch as he continues his close ties with JERRY WENTWORTH, San Leandro, Calif., who has been involved in these activities in the past."

The two scant references to Wentworth provoked many questions. Why did Barbara believe Wentworth had been recruited? How did Laura know he was involved in espionage? Can't they tell us more? What does the navy say?

Sparse though the reports were, they nevertheless represented exciting intelligence well worth exploiting, and Smits at once initiated a search. San Leandro lies within the province of the satellite FBI office in Oakland. So the FBI assigned

69

an Oakland agent, Robert Griego, to trace Wentworth.

Griego was a popular agent, quiet and darkly handsome. In any setting, he preferred to listen rather than talk. No one could recall having heard him raise his voice, disparage anybody, or seriously complain about anything. He had spent seven years in criminal investigations and the last three in counterintelligence. A succession of supervisors saw him as a methodical investigator who got done whatever he was asked to do. He undertook pedestrian and challenging tasks with equal willingness and seemed to enjoy whatever he did. Prosecutors delighted in working with him, because he understood the law so well and how to marshal and order the evidence they needed.

The oldest of five children, Griego grew up in Omaha, Nebraska, where his father practiced law. His mother was of Czech parentage, his father of Spanish descent. They prized their children above all else and nurtured them in a loving and disciplined home. At the University of Nebraska, Griego fell in love with and married a classmate, the daughter of an air force officer. After he finished Nebraska Law School and FBI training at Quantico, they were posted to San Francisco in 1975. His wife resumed her studies at the University of California, Berkeley, received a doctoral degree, and became a senior administrator at Mills College.

Griego at thirty-five was a happy man. He went to work eagerly and came home eagerly to a six-month-old son, an eight-year-old daughter, and a caring wife.

The morning he drove to San Leandro, he looked forward to being home early because he anticipated little difficulty in locating Wentworth. However, the name Jerry Wentworth did not appear in any telephone or street directory. He could not find the name on the tax rolls. The electric company had no record of Jerry Wentworth. The police had never heard of him. Neither had anyone else Griego approached in San Leandro.

He looked into surrounding areas, consulted the Naval District Headquarters in San Francisco, even had a friend inquire of the Navy League, all to no avail. Szady in Washington tried to help by forwarding a little more information from Barbara Walker. She had heard from her daughter Margaret that Wentworth might have retired from the navy and taken a job as a stockbroker. But so far as Griego could ascertain, in all of California there was no stockbroker named Jerry Wentworth. And if Wentworth in fact had retired from the navy, he now could be living anywhere in the United States or, for that matter, outside the United States.

By early May, Griego had to report that nowhere could he discern a single trace of Wentworth. The message published in the *Los Angeles Times* had elicited nothing from RUS. On all fronts, the investigation seemed stalled.

In Washington, though, there had been some progress. The Analytical Unit, studying and collating all available data, including a few more details from Barbara Walker, developed a hypothesis. Szady immediately communicated it to Smits in an urgent Top Secret teletype message: "Analytical Unit believes Wentworth may be RUS. More follows."

The Analytical Unit emphasized that the theory was just a theory, unsupported by any hard evidence. When Smits read the additional statements of Barbara Walker, he concluded that the theory was a very good one and fit many known facts of the case. In another interview, Barbara stated that she and Wentworth a number of times discussed the espionage activities of John Walker. Wentworth commented that he was reluctant to become entangled. But Barbara strongly believed that Wentworth eventually did involve himself, because he and Walker continued an unusually close relationship.

71

Though she had not seen Wentworth since 1976, from her children she understood that Walker frequently flew to California to see him and that Wentworth periodically traveled across the country to Norfolk.

Barbara described Wentworth as white, a navy enlisted man, possibly a chief petty officer, in his forties. She assumed but was not totally certain that, like Walker, he was a communications specialist. His wife, Brenda, was in her twenties, and Barbara thought she attended a college or university in the vicinity of Berkeley.

To Smits, the reasoning of the Analytical Unit now was clear and estimable. As communications specialists, Walker and Wentworth very well might have served together or met in the navy. As a communications specialist, Wentworth could have access to the keylists, technical manuals, and cryptographic material RUS said he passed to his contact. The presumed fact that Wentworth knew about Walker's spying but did not report it reflected a sorry character, the same type of amoral character that RUS through his letters had shown himself to be. Walker's business as a private investigator provided an ideal cover for a principal agent, or contact, to whom the RUS letters referred. The frequent meetings between Walker and Wentworth, each entailing a journey across the country and back, sounded as if they were conducted for more than social purposes. And they would explain both how RUS made deliveries to the contact and how Walker, without access to secrets himself, could continue to supply them to the Soviets.

Smits concluded that if the wife of Wentworth/RUS attended school near Berkeley, then he probably still lived nearby, retired or not. But where? By message, Smits pleaded with Szady for more details from Barbara and Laura Walker. San Francisco would welcome the least scrap.

On May 10 agents once more questioned Laura Walker, and

she did her very best. Despite considerable effort, she could neither find nor remember the address of Wentworth in San Leandro. However, she did recall for the agents the route she drove when she once visited the Wentworth apartment in 1982. Laura also remembered that twice in 1982 she had telephoned Wentworth. Happily, she had found his number among her papers.

Less than an hour after the FBI flashed the number to San Francisco, Griego dialed it and asked to speak to Jerry Wentworth. A male who answered told him he had the wrong number.

"I'm sorry," said Griego. "Jerry and I were shipmates. I'm sure this is the number he gave me. Have the Wentworths moved?"

The man testily declared that no one by the name of Wentworth was there and that the previous occupants of the house were not the Wentworths. He hung up.

The telephone company stated to Griego that the telephone number had been reassigned to a new customer. It claimed that its records did not reveal the name and address of the subscriber who previously had the number. Griego did obtain the address of the man who presently had the number and by neighborhood investigation determined he was not Wentworth. Again, no one had ever heard of Wentworth.

The FBI report outlining the route Laura Walker followed to Wentworth's apartment said:

> She drove north from Hayward, Calif., on Route 17 to the Washington Boulevard exit. She then made a left turn, which took her back over the freeway. LAURA believes this road is possibly Marina Boulevard. LAURA advised she continued on this road approximately three miles, passing a sign for the post office (on the right) and a Dairy Queen (on the left side of the road). After traveling three miles, she made a left turn and proceeded one or two blocks to an intersection. At the intersection

73

and parallel to Marina Boulevard was a road which had a grassy median. She recalls the WENTWORTH apartment has fencing or a small brick wall which outlines the parking area directly behind the building.

Following the directions, Griego tried for two days to locate the Wentworth apartment, and he discovered a building that bore some but not much similarity to the one Laura described. The manager assured him no Wentworth had lived there, at least not during the past five years.

At Quantico one of Griego's instructors had stressed the necessity of persistence in investigations. "It's always that last place you look that you find what you're looking for. Don't become discouraged. Use your imagination and keep looking."

Maybe, Griego thought, Wentworth might show up in an old telephone directory, and his former address might lead to his present one. Rummaging through office files, Griego found, instead of a telephone directory, a 1982 crisscross directory, which listed San Leandro telephone numbers together with names and addresses of subscribers. Alongside the number Laura Walker had retrieved was the name Jerry A. *Whitworth*.

Hastily, the FBI asked Laura if she might be mistaken about Jerry's last name. Could it be Whitworth? Now she remembered. Yes, she said, it very well might be Whitworth.

From records of the California Motor Vehicles Registry, Griego ascertained that Jerry Alfred Whitworth, driver's license number KOO57374, lived at 118 Full Circle Drive, Davis, California. He drove directly into San Francisco to report personally to Smits.

Smits smiled and summoned Peterson. "Congratulations," he said to Griego. "I think you've found RUS." Noting Griego's quizzical reaction, Smits realized FBI compartmentalization was such that Griego knew nothing about the RUS letters and little about the Walker case in Virginia.

They gave him copies of the letters, explained the Analytical Unit's theory, and briefed him about John Walker. "There's no proof that Wentworth or Whitworth and RUS are the same," Smits acknowledged. "But they smell like the same animal." He then announced that henceforth Griego would work out of the San Francisco office with Peterson.

"Should we talk to Whitworth?" Griego asked.

"No!" Smits emphatically declared. "For the time being, we can't go near him. John, see what the navy says."

The navy did have a complete service record of Jerry Alfred Whitworth, born August 10, 1939, Muldrow, Oklahoma. The summary San Francisco received indicated that Whitworth enlisted September 1962 and retired as a senior chief petty officer October 31, 1983. During the last ten years of service, he was assigned to supervisory duties pertaining to communications and cryptography at shore stations and aboard ships, including two aircraft carriers.

Examining the list of Whitworth's duty stations and assignments, Smits called out, "Here it is, John. Look." He pointed to a notation:

20 Oct 70–30 Jan 73
NTC, San Diego, CA
Instructor, Communications Schools Dept, Practical Application Laboratory
Instructor, Communications Quality Monitoring Course

Then Smits displayed an excerpt from John Walker's service record on his computer screen. It showed that for some eighteen months in 1970 and 1971, Walker was the chief instructor of the classes that Whitworth taught at the Naval Training Center in San Diego.

"You see," said Smits. "Walker was Whitworth's boss."

Much of the navy jargon and many of the abbreviations denoting Whitworth's assignments mystified Smits, and he asked Peterson if from his marine background he understood them.

"Some," Peterson replied. "I know what 'CMS Custodian' means, for example."

"What?"

"Literally, it means Classified Material Systems Custodian. He's the guy in charge of all the keylists, tech manuals, and other crypto stuff on the ship. He's responsible for the security of it all, for issuing what's needed when needed."

"He has access to everything?"

"Access! Hell, I told you, it's *his*. He keeps it in a vault or a safe and controls it all. No one can come near it except him."

"God!"

"I know."

The summary disclosed that at two duty stations, Whitworth had been custodian of all the navy's cryptographic materials. Locked in a vault immune from interruption, much less detection, he could have photographed all the keylists or ciphers, all the manuals diagramming the cryptographic machines used not only by the navy but by the army, air force, CIA, FBI, and State Department as well.

Within the investigative limitations laid down by Smits, Griego could not determine the nature of Whitworth's current employment, if any. Almost certainly he was not a stockbroker. Disguised inquiries did establish that a Brenda Reis was a graduate student at the University of California, Davis. Brenda Reis was the maiden name of Whitworth's wife. Unquestionably, Wentworth was Whitworth.

On Friday morning, May 17, 1985, Smits conferred with Peterson and Griego. He began with a summary from a legalistic point of view. There was not a scintilla of legal evidence against Whitworth. Granted, Barbara and Laura Walker were sincere sources who had supplied invaluable information. But their memory of events transpiring years ago might be fallible. After all, they had not correctly remembered Whitworth's name. In support of their suspicions about Whitworth, they cited the belief that he and Walker met frequently. But that belief was based mainly on hearsay. Obviously, John Walker and Whitworth knew each other, and maybe they were friends. Just as obviously, not every friend or associate of Walker was a spy.

Whitworth long held Top Secret and Cryptographic security clearances. Presumably, the navy issued and renewed them only after thorough investigations of his background. His service record contained nothing derogatory. On the contrary, Smits continued, it portrayed a citizen who for more than two decades had served the country honorably and well in sensitive and demanding positions. While the known background of Whitworth certainly matched the profile the FBI had drawn of RUS, again there was no proof.

"Come on, Count," Peterson irreverently interrupted. "You don't believe any of that."

"No," Smits replied evenly. "I am merely clarifying part of our problem."

The other part of the problem arose from the customs and practices of FBI bureaucracy. Davis, California, falls within the jurisdiction of the FBI's Sacramento office, which therefore had territorial rights to the case. The Sacramento office was a relatively small one, without a separate counterintelligence unit. In consequence of the FBI practice of posting beginning agents to small offices, most of its agents were young and inexperienced.

That did not mean they were not good. One of the most promising agents with whom Smits ever worked was a striking young Japanese-American woman who came to the San Francisco office with a master's degree from Stanford University. Only a few months before, Smits fiercely if unsuccessfully had resisted her transfer to Los Angeles.

But if Whitworth was a spy, then he demonstrably was a very good one who for years had made a mockery of American security. The young agents would have to watch and gather evidence without alerting him. The anachronistic premise that any agent could accomplish any mission, trained for it or not, had cost the FBI dearly in the past.

Therefore, Smits proposed a diplomatic expedition to Sacramento to persuade the agent in charge there to enter into a joint venture with the San Francisco office. Without infringing on Sacramento's prerogatives, he would offer counterintelligence expertise and manpower as needed.

"I want you both along," Smits said.

"When do we go?" Peterson asked.

"Sooner the better," Smits said. "I'll call right now." By telephone, he scheduled a meeting in Sacramento for 10:00 A.M. on Monday, May 20. By teletype, he advised headquarters of his operational intentions.

It was about 1:00 P.M. and, as Peterson suggested, time for lunch. Smits said he would send for sandwiches and they could keep talking.

"I'm tired of ersatz turkey," Peterson protested. "Let's have a decent meal at Phnom Penh." A dozen or so people were lined up outside the restaurant, but the sunlit afternoon was magnificent, and Peterson stepped inside to say they were waiting for a table.

Within a minute, his friend the tiny waiter appeared and ushered them inside past glowering patrons who had been waiting for some time. To them the waiter apologized, "He book table last week."

Peterson ordered a Chinese beer, Smits a Coke; Griego hesitated. "Make it three beers," Peterson told the waiter.

They agreed to rendezvous at 8:30 A.M. Monday outside San Francisco for the drive to Sacramento. Smits remarked that over the weekend maybe they all should take their wives to dinner. "This may be our last free weekend for quite a while."

About the same time, give or take an hour, Joe Wolfinger in Norfolk picked up intelligence that was to make Smits's estimate very prophetic.

5

"It's Incredible"

JOHN WALKER for more than six weeks completely frustrated FBI monitors trying to glean clues from his telephone conversations. They heard a lot of colorful and frequently filthy language from Walker, who uttered such bons mots as: "If I found a man in bed with my wife, I'd just laugh at the asshole." "You could get 'em a blow job by [a movie star] and they'd bitch about it because they bitch about everything." "He'll just ramble on endlessly about not being able to get laid." Walker disparaged women in general, habitually referring to them as "dumb cunts." Of one in particular he said, "She's such an airhead you have to tie her down to keep her from floating away." He spoke the most obscene blasphemies, sometimes adding, "God will forgive me. He has a sense of humor."

Walker exhibited much pride in himself and his work as a private investigator. When someone suggested he should consider more sedate or prestigious employment, he replied: "Quit! Would a brain surgeon quit to become a taxi driver? I'm a pro. I'm the best there is. I love surveillance. I'd rather be on a surveillance than screwing [some beauty queen]."

Although they learned something about Walker personally,

the monitors heard not a single incriminating word, not a hint of espionage, nothing that furthered the investigation. At headquarters the dearth of leads from the telephone intercepts and spot surveillances revived arguments that the FBI was confronted by an old or dead case.

However, on Friday, May 17, the intercepts finally yielded possibly significant intelligence. One of Walker's aunts had died in Pennsylvania, and her funeral was scheduled on Sunday. Apparently, the aunt had been a surrogate mother to Walker, virtually raising him. Yet he informed relatives that on Sunday urgent business in North Carolina would preclude him from attending the funeral. A relative called back, imploring him to delay the business or appoint someone else to take care of it. Walker was adamant; the business could not be postponed, and only he could attend to it.

His inflexibility intrigued Wolfinger and Hunter. FBI observations indicated that Walker normally did not work on Sundays. In none of the monitored conversations had he talked about having to do anything this coming Sunday. It was not unusual for him to farm out jobs to associates or employees. What business was so vital that it had to be transacted this Sunday, and only by him? What would compel him to ignore the funeral of a woman who had been closer to him than his natural mother?

"I guess if he means to work Sunday, we'll just have to work too," Wolfinger said.

On Sunday morning Walker paused after stepping from his two-story house in suburban Norfolk. He scanned the quiet street in front and then climbed into his new 1985 Chevrolet Astro van. In addition to his familiar toupee, gold-rimmed glasses, beard, and mustache, he wore a dark blue pullover shirt, blue jeans, a black nylon windbreaker, and casual shoes. The watchers thought maybe he had dressed for comfort while driving and intended to change clothes at his destination.

Meandering westward through the city, Walker seemed in no hurry. Twice he stopped, as if to peruse a map or find something in the glove compartment; once he turned into a driveway, backed out, and reversed direction. The maneuvers, executed to detect surveillance, demonstrated clearly to the FBI agents that they were tracking a professional and had better keep their distance.

Members of the surveillance team communicated with one another and reported to Wolfinger in the command car via radio telephones equipped with scramblers. Outside Norfolk, an agent shouted into his microphone an electrifying report: Walker was turning not south toward North Carolina but northward on Interstate 64.

Some six months earlier, Wolfinger had quit smoking, cold turkey. He had overcome the physical agonies of withdrawal and daily resisted psychological temptations to renew the addiction. To prove to himself the power of his will, he purposely left cigars in the car. Now he involuntarily reached into the glove compartment and began to smoke again. The turn northward meant that Walker might be heading toward the Washington area, that the FBI at last might have its chance. At the moment, nothing else except that chance mattered to him.

From the accounts of Barbara Walker, it was clear that prior to 1976, at least, the Washington residency of either the GRU or KGB serviced Walker. Even after moving to California, he continued to deliver and receive materials at drops around Washington. Certainly, in subsequent years the Soviets might have arranged to meet or effect exchanges with him elsewhere. But Szady and Wolfinger reasoned that if Walker still was active, one of the Washington residencies still might be handling him. Accordingly, the FBI had made contingency plans for a massive surveillance should he ever come near Washington.

At Hampton, Virginia, Wolfinger stopped and from a phone booth called the Washington field office. "Wind Flyer [the FBI code name for the Walker case] may be coming your way. He's proceeding north toward Richmond on Interstate 64."

About the time Wolfinger called, A. Jackson Lowe was preparing to paint his small sailboat. A tall, fair, blue-eyed gentleman from the mountains of southwestern Virginia, Jack Lowe belonged to the bright FBI class of '72. He had worked in counterintelligence since 1974 and was regarded as one of the bureau's most astute analysts of Soviet clandestine operations. Shortly after 2:00 P.M., Lowe's beeper sounded a coded signal, which translated to "Walker is moving." Simultaneously, beepers transmitted the same signal to some sixty-five other FBI agents and civilian employees.

At the Montclair Country Club near Quantico, Virginia, an attendant dashed across the golf course, found David Szady, and told him to call his office immediately. By phone a duty officer announced to him, "Wind Flyer Command Center has been activated."

The contingency plan provided for a command center at the Washington field office, which has more elaborate facilities for operational communications than does headquarters. As Szady raced to the field office in his golf clothes, he laughed at a paradox about which others frequently cursed.

In 1974 the State Department gave the Soviet Union the choicest site in Washington on which to construct a new embassy and apartment building for its diplomatic (and espionage) personnel. Known as Mount Alto, the site is literally the highest point in Washington. It is secure, lovely, and convenient to almost everything of interest in the city. And from the heights of Mount Alto the Soviets can focus microwave and other eavesdropping beams upon the principal government offices of the capital.

By contrast, in 1976 the FBI's Washington field office had to vacate the centrally located Old Post Office Building, which was being renovated to help beautify Pennsylvania Avenue. The field office wound up in a grimly graceless building situated on one of the lowest and most squalid sites in all Washington. The building was empty because no other government agency would occupy it. Isolated in a southwest Washington ghetto area, it is adjacent to the polluted Anacostia River, on which sewage and an occasional body float by; a cement factory; a power plant; and Washington's largest gay bar. Neighboring streets are poorly maintained and pocked with potholes that exact a heavy toll on shock absorbers. The neighborhood itself is unsafe for women at night, bereft of dining and parking facilities, and far away from everything of concern to the FBI, including the Soviet embassy.

Taking charge of the command center at about 2:45 P.M., Szady learned that a surveillance aircraft was airborne and two more were on standby. Meanwhile, Washington agents and civilians from the special surveillance group deployed southward in twenty automobiles.

The operational plan called for them to take over the surveillance from the Norfolk team once Walker came within twenty-five miles of Washington. The Norfolk agent now following Walker was Beverly Andress, the young agent who so adroitly dealt with Barbara Walker. Her radio malfunctioned, and though she could hear the Washington contingent desperately asking for directions, she could not respond.

Finally, at 3:20 P.M., near Woodbridge, Virginia, she got through long enough to guide Washington agents to Walker's

84

white van. Eleven seconds later, her radio burst into flames. She had to swerve off the highway and jump from the car. Eleven seconds had made a great difference.

Vectored by radio from surveillance cars, the aircraft located Walker and at 3:45 P.M. reported to the command center that he was heading northwest on Interstate 495, which encircles Washington. Shortly after crossing the Potomac River into Maryland at about 4:00 P.M., he veered off Interstate 495 and drove into the rural woodlands of Montgomery County. There, he began wandering up and down empty lanes and narrow roads that led nowhere except to isolated farmhouses. He made sharp turns, doubled back, and several times stopped the van, got out, and looked around, seemingly at nothing.

The periodic reports of his movements radioed by Jack Lowe, who was supervising the surveillance on the scene, eradicated all doubts. Indisputably, the case was live. Everyone understood that Walker was both guarding against surveillance and reconnoitering, familiarizing himself with signal and drop sites.

Having arrived at the command center, Wolfinger and Hunter listened to Szady jubilantly announce Lowe's reports. But about 5:00 P.M., Szady silently stared down at his desk while composing himself.

"What's the matter, Z-man?" someone asked.

"We've lost him. Jack says he's gone."

Because of all the twists and turns in the maze of empty roads Walker followed, the surveillants could not keep him constantly in sight without exposing themselves. They had to rely upon the aircraft to maintain visual contact and to direct the cars safely ahead of and behind him. When Walker slipped into an area shielded from the sky by the thick spring foliage of the trees, he became invisible to the plane. The inability of ground units to locate him in the woods and the aircraft to sight him on any of the adjacent open roads suggested he had left the area.

Careful not to show his own discouragement and alarm, Szady rejected Lowe's apologies. "It's not your fault. You had it right. Go ahead and stick with the plan."

In the contingency planning, Lowe had expressly envisioned the possibility of losing Walker. Given the overriding necessity of not allowing him to detect the surveillance, the possibility was strong. The nature of the area — roughly twenty square miles — he traversed that afternoon made it still stronger.

Lowe reflected upon Barbara Walker's narrative of her excursion with Walker into the northern Virginia countryside sixteen years earlier. They flew from California to Washington, registered at a motel in Fairfax, Virginia, and in the afternoon drove into the countryside, where Walker twice left the car and went into the woods. After dark they returned. At one of the places they had stopped in the afternoon, Walker deposited a sack filled with trash and film. An hour or so later at another, he picked up a package containing thirty-five thousand dollars.

Lowe concluded that if Walker escaped the surveillance, the FBI should gamble that he would repeat the 1969 procedures and come back later. Accordingly, Lowe dispersed the watchers and hid them along the routes Walker had traveled, instructing them to do nothing but wait. Szady sent a second aircraft to relieve the first, whose fuel now was depleted.

Logically, the strategy was sound. If Walker had been surveying sites, he obviously meant to use them eventually. Nevertheless, as hours passed and darkness gathered, apprehensions mounted.

Then, shortly after 8:00 P.M., Szady heard Lowe's mellifluous Virginia accent. "We have him, Z-man! He's coming back on Glen Mill Road just like he did this afternoon."

"Congratulations!"

"Well, if the creek don't rise and the Lord be willing, we'll stay with him this time."

Near a crossroads formed by Branch, Circle, and Ridge drives, Walker parked, left the van, and appeared to look for something before driving on at 8:19 P.M.

At 8:20 P.M. Agent James Kolouch, who was in the car with Lowe, radioed a dramatic report. A 1983 blue Malibu sedan bearing license number DSX144 was entering the area. One minute later, another surveillant advised that it was driven by a man accompanied by a woman and child.

The *DSX* signified that the car was registered to a Soviet diplomat; the *144* denoted a name. The computer system installed by Wolfinger quickly yielded the name of Aleksei Gavrilovich Tkachenko, since January 1983 third secretary of the Soviet embassy; he had been positively identified as a KGB officer but marked down as a low-level administrator of only nominal interest.

Thoughts flashed before Szady like images on a computer screen. *Okay, it's a KGB operation, not GRU. It shouldn't be my case. But it is mine, to win or lose. Okay, we screwed up and let the Sovs disguise Tkachenko from us. We can worry about that later. Right now they're going to load and unload drops. Walker's got something for them. This is our chance. For them it's very big. That's why they're risking the wife and kid as decoys.*

Darkness now sided with the FBI. Walker's headlights facilitated the surveillance both on the ground and from the air, and the watchers kept theirs off. At 8:30 P.M. they saw Walker leave the van by a field near the intersection of Dufief Mill and Quince Orchard roads and walk around a utility pole. After he departed, Lowe searched around the pole and found a 7-Up soft drink can on which an orange dot had been painted.

To the KGB and the FBI the can said: I understand your last instructions. I am in the area. I will deliver material to my drop. I will retrieve material from your drop in accordance with the schedule you stipulated. I have no reason to believe the area is unsafe.

Covering his hand with his shirt, Lowe picked up the can, made sure it was empty, and put it back down so Tkachenko would see it and proceed with the operation.

By radio, Lowe reported the discovery and location of the can to the surveillance team as a whole. As an afterthought he added, "Remember. Don't let's forget about that can. It should have fingerprints, so it's evidence." A trailing squad misinterpreted the admonition, swept in, and grabbed the can.

Concentrating upon Walker and hunting for sites where he and Tkachenko would make their actual drops, the surveillants temporarily lost track of the KGB officer. There is little question, though, about what happened. At the signal site, Tkachenko could not find the can. To him, its absence meant either that Walker had been unable to adhere to the operational schedule or that he had sensed danger and fled. In any case, Tkachenko had to abort the operation and flee himself. At 9:08 P.M. a squad saw him speeding out of the area on River Road.

Meanwhile, Walker repeated his movements of the afternoon, and about four miles from the signal site stopped near the intersection of Partnership and Whites Ferry roads. Next to a huge tree on which a No Hunting sign was posted, he loitered around a utility pole for a minute or so. He returned to the van, furtively looked up and down the road, then drove out of the area.

While some surveillants followed him to a suburban shopping center where he seemed to do nothing but pass time, others searched around the pole. At 9:41 P.M. they found a large grocery sack containing beneath some trash a horde of secret documents.

"Don't take time to study them or count them," Szady ordered. "Get them to headquarters at once."

Szady immediately telephoned John Dion, chief of the Espionage Prosecutions Unit of the Justice Department's Internal Security Section. "Remember that matter I discussed with you last week? Well, it's happening right now. We need you at headquarters."

Like Szady, Dion came from Massachusetts and a loving Catholic family. His father was a factory worker, his mother a schoolteacher. Though their combined income was modest, they always saved for their son's college education.

As a boy, Dion thrilled to the Notre Dame victory march, and the day Notre Dame accepted him as a student was the proudest of his adolescence. After graduation, he studied law at George Washington University and upon receipt of his degree joined the Justice Department.

Espionage long had fascinated him, and when he learned that a position in the Internal Security Section was open, he applied for it. The chief, John L. Martin, chose him from among scores of applicants, and as the subsequent record demonstrates, the two soon formed one of the most effective partnerships in government. Under Martin, Dion had helped plan the arrests and prosecution of more than twenty spies. FBI agents trusted him because he understood espionage and tried to advise them how to do legally what they needed to do in investigations.

At his home in McLean, Virginia, Dion hurriedly said good night to his two small children and pretty, freckled wife, Tina, who had been a law school classmate. Tall, slender, his wavy dark hair uncombed, in blue jeans and a Notre Dame sweat-shirt, he looked like a youthful scholar off on a field trip.

Rodney Leffler, deputy chief of the FBI's Soviet Section, and Jerry Richards, the espionage expert in the FBI laboratory, already were waiting at the headquarters building on Pennsylvania Avenue when Dion arrived. About 10:45 P.M. two FBI agents wearing camouflaged battle fatigues rushed into the office with the documents.

Their sheer number, 129 in all, initially overwhelmed. As Richards spread them out on desks and tables, Leffler, a veteran of many years in counterintelligence, exclaimed, "I've never seen anything like this." The Soviets would have prized any one of the deciphered secret messages or classified manuals. Yet here in a single batch were 129!

The origin of the documents most struck Dion. Most, if not all, clearly came from the aircraft carrier *Nimitz,* on which Walker's twenty-three-year-old son, Michael, was serving as a seaman. "It's Michael," Dion said ruefully. "I should have seen it. He tried to suborn his daughter. Why not his son?"

More portentous than the documents themselves was a typed letter found among them. Obviously written by Walker to the KGB, it said:

Dear Friend,

This delivery consists of material from "S" and is similar to the previously supplied material. The quantity is limited, unfortunately, due to his operating schedule and increased security prior to deployment. His ship departed in early March, and they operated extensively just prior to deployment. The situation around him looks very good, and he is amassing a vast amount of material right now. His last correspondence indicated that he now has material that would fill two large grocery bags. Storage is becoming a problem. As is obvious, I did not make a trip to Europe to pick up material for this delivery.

His schedule does fit fairly well with our meeting, and I plan to meet him during a port call which will give me two days to make it to our meeting. I will arrange to pick up the best of his material and deliver it in bulk; photographing it on the road does not seem practical. Also, the entire amount he has would be impossible to safely transport, and I plan to deliver that at the schedule you will provide. I hope his ship doesn't experience a schedule change which will put me in the same situation we once faced in Hong Kong — I did not make the primary date, and we met on the alternate. So I have a decision to make, and here it is: If his schedule changes and I cannot make the Primary date, I will collect the material and make the Secondary date.

"D" continues to be a puzzle. He is not happy but is still not ready to continue our "cooperation." Rather than try to analyze him for you, I have simply enclosed portions of two letters I've received. My guess? He is going to flop in the stockbroker field and can probably make a modest living in computer sales. He has become accustomed to the big spender lifestyle, and I don't believe he will adjust to living off his wife's income. He will attempt to renew cooperation within two years.

"F" has been transferred and is in a temporary situation giving him no access at all. He is having difficulty in making a career decision in the navy. He is not happy and is experiencing family pressure with [his] father, who is 73 and in poor health. He married (his father) a younger woman who has a significant drinking problem. "F" feels obligated to support them. He may come around, and good access is possible.

"K" and I have discussed your proposal, and I will pass on some extensive details when we meet. Briefly, he is involved in carrier and amphibious ship maintenance planning. He would instantly recognize unrealistic repair schedules or see that ships were "off their normal schedules." This may provide a basis for the information we seek. Otherwise, he has no useful material.

So I will see you as scheduled and hope I will make the Primary date with no problem. I'm sure you have access to S's port schedule and can anticipate my moves in advance. I am not providing his schedule in this note for obvious reasons.
Good luck. . . .

"S" clearly was Michael Walker, who was "amassing a vast amount" of secrets for the Soviets. The references to "D," together with an enclosed excerpt from a letter in which D mentioned his wife, Brenda, made clear that he was Jerry Whitworth, alias RUS. "F" at the moment was a mystery. "K" probably was Arthur Walker, whose employer, the VSE Corporation, advised the navy regarding ship maintenance and repairs.

Walker was masterminding a whole spy ring, just as RUS said his contact was doing. And this had been going on for seventeen years!

At that very moment, Walker was back in the countryside frantically attempting to serve the KGB and comply with its instructions. He had returned to the general area of the drops about 10:15, and near the intersection of Old Bucklodge Lane and White Ground Road appeared to search for something on the ground behind two ancient trees. Finding nothing, he drove a short distance, stopped, turned on the interior lights of the van, and studied a map. He drove back to the trees and this time used a flashlight to search the ground, an action that bespoke desperation to the two FBI agents lurking ten yards away. Failing again, he sped to the site where he had left the sack with the documents and saw that it was gone.

Now he was confused and alarmed. If the KGB had picked up the documents, then a package should have been left for him by the two trees. Had the KGB decided for some reason not to place it there, then the package should have been put at the site where Walker left the sack. And throughout many years, the KGB had never fouled up drop procedures. Like a man who discovers that his wallet is missing, Walker simply could not believe it. So he kept shuttling back and forth between the two sites, hoping to find what Tkachenko had not delivered.

About 11:30 P.M. Rod Leffler radioed Lowe. "You have authority to arrest Walker without a warrant."

"How come?" asked Lowe, who always had been warned of the legal risks of warrantless arrests.

"Jack, this package you sent; it's incredible. It's just incredible. John Dion has given the authority. So arrest him."

"I have to coordinate with Z-man."

"All right. Go ahead. But whatever you do, arrest him at all costs. Don't let him escape."

By now, a frustrated Walker had given up for the evening and headed out toward Rockville, Maryland. Aware that Walker had a permit to carry a weapon and assuming that he was armed, Szady and Lowe decided against halting him on the highway. If at all possible, they wanted to take him instantly by surprise.

At the Ramada Inn in Rockville, Walker carefully parked his new van away from other vehicles and entered the motel. Scrambling from their cars, some FBI agents surrounded the building, while others rushed in to seize him in the lobby. He was nowhere to be seen; not in the lobby, restroom, stairwell, or bar.

With the help of motel personnel and by consulting the guest registry, the agents ascertained that Walker had checked in earlier, doubtless during the hours the FBI lost him, under the name Johnson. They missed him in the lobby because he had gone directly to his room, 763. William O'Keefe, the agent in charge of the arrest, decided that now there was time to regroup and plan.

In accordance with FBI tradition, Szady sent Bob Hunter,

the first agent assigned to the case, to the motel so he could have the honor of making the arrest.

Walker liked to boast that if he had to die, he wanted to die in a gunfight. Though Hunter and Jim Kolouch periodically underwent firearms training, they were not gunfighters. They were dead-tired men in their forties. Kolouch's specialty was accounting, and he had been in counterintelligence only two years. But as Hunter and Kolouch put on flak vests in Room 750, they made a solemn pact. If necessary, they would let Walker fire the first shot; they would risk death to capture him alive. The United States had to know what only he could tell.

At 3:30 A.M. Hunter and Kolouch positioned themselves in a corridor around the corner from the elevator bank, which was near Room 763. From the lobby, Agent Billy Wang, posing as a room clerk, telephoned and apologetically informed Walker that a drunk driver had crashed into his van. Could he please come down and straighten out the insurance matters?

Walker warily stepped out, checked the stairwell, then darted back into his room. Some minutes later, Hunter and Kolouch heard his door open. Revolvers drawn, they ran around the corner to confront Walker, who was pointing a blue steel .38-caliber revolver straight at them.

"FBI! Drop it!"

From a range of no more than five yards, they faced for five, maybe ten seconds, which seemed much longer. Cunning as ever, Walker calculated. He could get off one shot, not two. Grinning, he let the revolver slip from his right hand.

Kolouch slammed him against the wall, handcuffed him, and ripped off his toupee, glasses, belt, shoes, and socks. Heart pounding, Hunter announced, "You are under arrest for violation of the espionage laws of the United States."

In the motel parking lot, sirens wailed, lights flashed, and dozens of agents, some in combat gear, some in the Sunday dress they had on when summoned an eternity ago, crowded around. Manacled and shorn of his hairpiece and glasses, Walker reminded them of a snarling animal, trapped but untamed. His little, predatory eyes stared at the agents contemptuously, and he sneered at them.

"Quite a crowd you've got here. Don't you have any consideration for the taxpayers? And that phony call. That's the oldest trick in the book."

"It may be an old trick, Mr. Walker," said Billy Wang. "But you now are with us."

Jack Lowe commanded, "Get in the car, Mr. Walker, else I will have to assist you."

At FBI headquarters, John Dion, Rod Leffler, and Jerry Richards enjoyed no sense of triumph. There had not been time fully to assess the magnitude of what had been unveiled. There simply was too much to do. Smits in San Francisco, the navy, the White House, the National Security Agency, the National Security Council, the attorney general, the director of the FBI, all had to be notified. Spies S, D, K, and perhaps others were still at large. Yet Dion, Leffler, and Richards had seen enough to recognize unmistakable indications of a national catastrophe.

Around 4:00 A.M. Dion called to inform his boss, John Martin, of the arrest. Because they were not speaking over secure telephones, they talked elliptically. Referring to the damage reflected by the documents and papers recovered from the drop, Martin asked, "How bad is it?"

"It's bad, John," Dion told him. "Like Rod says, it's incredible."

They closed the command center around 5:00 A.M. Szady would go to headquarters, Wolfinger straight back to Norfolk to organize the searches of Walker's home, boat, and airplane.

Of those who long had doubted Barbara and Laura Walker, Wolfinger remarked, "Z-man, it's a bad day for the skeptics."

Wearily and grimly, Szady shook his head. "It's also a bad day for the country."

"Yes, it is."

6

Unraveling the Net

I N PREDAWN MISTS outside San Francisco, Smits rendezvoused with Peterson and Griego for the drive to Sacramento. He related to them what he had learned from
Szady about the arrest of John Walker and outlined the new
strategy it necessitated. They no longer could investigate and
gather evidence against Jerry Whitworth without his knowledge. News of the arrest would alert him, and he very well
might try to flee the country.

Now they had nothing to lose by confronting him head-on
and trying to shock him into confession. With luck, they might
beard him before he heard and had time to compose himself.
In any case, Peterson together with a Sacramento agent would
go straight in once Whitworth's wife, Brenda, left. Griego and
a Sacramento agent, preferably a female, would wait outside
to intercept and question Brenda should she return during the
interrogation of Whitworth.

Meanwhile, Sacramento agents hid themselves around
Whitworth's mobile home, anchored in a trailer park at Davis,
California. In Norfolk, Wolfinger's agents ringed John Walker's house pending receipt of a search warrant. From Suit-
land, Maryland, the Naval Investigative Service flashed messages to the captain of the USS *Nimitz,* moored at Haifa,

Israel, and to Naval Investigative Service agent Keith Hitt, based in Rome. And in Washington, inside a seedy building on Ninth Street N.W. near porno shops, Dion began briefing the head of the Justice Department's Internal Security Section, John Martin, to whom control of all the developing cases soon would pass.

John Martin stands six feet three inches tall, has the handsome, photogenic face of a matinee idol, bears himself with the confidence of a man in control, and exudes enthusiasm. From Israel to Taiwan, the Glienicke Bridge in Berlin to the backwaters of Mississippi, the United States often has entrusted him with sensitive missions and responsibilities. He earned the trust of his own and many foreign governments by sheer incorruptible merit.

Born into a family of ten children in Utica, New York, Martin worked his way through college, won a full scholarship to Syracuse University Law School, and entered the FBI in 1962.

In June of 1964, three young civil rights workers — two from the North and the third a Mississipian — were murdered in Neshoba County, Mississippi. In the climate of the time, the killings posed, symbolically and actually, landmark challenges. Could black people rely upon newly enacted civil rights laws to afford them justice and freedom from terrorism? Could the FBI amass enough evidence to convince Southern white juries to convict?

Martin participated in the investigation that uncovered the bodies of the three victims buried in a recently constructed earthen dam. The investigators identified numerous Ku Klux Klansmen as suspects and Martin helped in the arrests. Ultimately, eight men were convicted and imprisoned.

From civil rights investigations, the FBI transferred Martin to counterintelligence, and in 1965 it made him one of the youngest headquarters supervisors in bureau history. He received awards and commendations from J. Edgar Hoover personally, and his career prospects were bright.

But Martin never intended to make the FBI his career. He joined it, as many people join the military, to fulfill a patriotic duty. Always, he had pledged that he would prove to himself that he could make his own way outside government, and in 1968 he went into private law practice. He welcomed the money it brought but not the necessity of representing clients in whose cause he was uninterested. He found that nothing in private practice satisfied him as much as representing the United States, that nothing was as much fun as hunting spies and murderers had been. When the Justice Department in the summer of 1971 offered him a supervisory job, he accepted without hesitation.

The forty-two months of private practice, however, gave Martin some assurances. He knew that in government, as elsewhere, you cannot truly serve superiors by obsequity, by telling them what they want to hear rather than unpleasant facts they often need to hear. To really do your job, you have to be willing to risk it at any time. That he was prepared to do. At any time, he could quit the government and double his income in private practice.

Through a double-agent operation, the FBI in 1978 wove an iron web of espionage evidence around two KGB officers who were employed by the United Nations and did not have diplomatic immunity. The State Department tried to prevent their arrest on grounds that the ensuing fuss would impair relations with the Soviet Union. The CIA, under Admiral Stansfield Turner, curiously aligned itself with the State Department, contending that arrests would only provoke Soviet retaliation. To Attorney General Griffin Bell, Martin laid down countervailing arguments. The position of the State Department and

CIA mocked the whole FBI counterintelligence effort. Usually when a KGB officer was caught in flagrante, he enjoyed diplomatic status and could not be prosecuted. Here were two Russians who could be prosecuted. To let them quietly go home merely would invite contempt from the Soviets, embolden them to intensify espionage, and in effect cede to them the right to make or nullify U.S. law. Bell, an honest, unaffected Georgia lawyer, agreed. He announced they would take the issue directly to President Carter.

Having listened to the opposing arguments, the president on a Saturday morning angrily ordered the two KGB men arrested. In the eyes of the bureaucracy, he thereby established an important precedent: Henceforth, whenever legally possible and operationally practicable, Soviet spies would be prosecuted.

Justice Department subordinates in 1979 confidentially confronted Martin with a difficult professional and moral decision. They revealed that a sensitive operation had learned that Billy Carter, brother of the president, was taking money from Libyan dictator Muammar Qadaffi. At least one specific payment of $200,000 had been documented. This intelligence had been disseminated to a limited number of officials, but thus far it had been suppressed, and the FBI had not been notified.

Martin asked himself some questions. Did he as a civil servant have the right to expose a scandal that would embarrass the president personally? What would happen to him if he did? Would not silence better serve the overall national interest?

Within the hour, Martin answered the questions and resolved to back up his subordinates by spreading the facts before the Justice Department hierarchy, including Attorney General Benjamin Civiletti, who had succeeded Bell.

An investigation soon began. Though Billy Carter successfully pleaded that the money passed simply constituted a loan bestowed by a considerate lender upon a commercially worthy borrower, the public exposure precluded any possibility that Qadaffi might influence American policy through the president's brother.

Promoted to chief of the Internal Security Section in 1980, Martin inherited more responsibilities — secretly negotiating with the Soviets about prisoner exchanges; standing on the bridge in Berlin while the exchanges occurred; forging with allies new legal measures against terrorism; warning other allies, by word and deed, to cease clandestine activities in the United States.

But his main job remained the same as it had been since 1975, enforcement of the espionage statutes. Between 1966 and 1975 the United States successfully prosecuted only two espionage cases. Between 1975 and 1985 Martin presided over the successful prosecution of thirty-one people for spying, sixteen of them in 1984 and 1985 alone. And more cases were pending.

The successful prosecutions prompted the Associated Press to term Martin "the top U.S. spy hunter." He was the first to point out that the flattering reference was erroneous. He did not detect spies. The security services, principally the FBI, did the hunting, gathered the evidence, made the arrests. His duty was to make sure they received whatever legal advice they needed during an investigation, tell them when they had enough evidence, devise legal strategy, and oversee prosecutions. He and the weary Dion began to discuss such issues the morning of May 20.

At 11:30 that morning in California, John Peterson, accompanied by Special Agent Michael McElwee from Sacramento, knocked on Jerry Whitworth's door. A tall, fully bearded man wearing thick spectacles opened it. His thinning straight hair was a dingy dark brown, his face utterly plain. Peterson guessed he had grown the long beard to relieve or obscure the plainness.

Presenting their credentials, Peterson and McElwee introduced themselves as FBI agents. "We would like to ask you some questions."

"All right, come in."

Whitworth led them through a kind of den where he evidently had been writing a letter on a computer and invited them to sit at the dining room table.

"John Walker was arrested last night for espionage," Peterson announced. "Do you have any knowledge of his espionage activities?"

Hands trembling, Whitworth with difficulty managed to say in a choked voice, "No." Looking rapidly about the room, he stammered hoarsely, "I . . . I need a drink of water."

Whitworth walked into the kitchen, passed a bottled water dispenser, and stepped into the den. McElwee jumped up, followed, and saw him remove a floppy disc and a print-out from the computer and sequester them among equipment on a table. "Mr. Whitworth, for your safety and ours as well, it is necessary that you remain within our sight as long as we are here," McElwee said.

"Oh, of course."

Back in the dining room, Peterson told Whitworth, "We have reason to believe that you yourself are involved in espionage."

Whitworth slumped in his chair and trembled. "That's really heavy stuff," he muttered. Again it was hard for him to speak. "I'd really like to talk to someone, to explain. I'd like to explain if I could."

Following Supreme Court rulings, Peterson advised: "You do not have to talk to us. You have the right to remain silent. But if you do talk, anything you say may be used against you in a court of law. You have the right to an attorney. If you cannot afford to pay an attorney, one will be appointed to represent you free of charge. If you decide to talk to us, you have the right to stop the questioning at any time."

"I'd . . . I'd like to explain about me and Walker."

"First, read this," McElwee ordered, handing him a form entitled "Interrogation; Advice of Rights." Having waived his right to counsel and silence by signing the form, Whitworth embarked upon a meandering monologue about his relationship with John Walker.

The two first met in February 1971 in San Diego, where Walker was Whitworth's supervisor at a communications training laboratory. Whitworth very much liked to sail, Walker had a boat, and they sailed together virtually every weekend until Walker was transferred in the summer of 1972.

Nevertheless, they were not true friends. Whitworth considered Walker dishonest and a womanizer abusive of women. One weekend after Walker cursed in the presence of his girlfriend, Whitworth announced he no longer would sail with him. The next weekend Whitworth had a date with "an older, possessive woman." Disliking "older, possessive" women, Whitworth spent the entire weekend wishing he was sailing with Walker. He decided to "accept Johnny as he is" and resume sailing.

Even though he really did not like Walker, Whitworth continued to see him through the years. Once he visited him in Norfolk, and once Walker flew to California to visit.

Whitworth absolutely would not trust Walker with his wife or his "livelihood." However, he thought the United States government could safely trust him.

Peterson thought both the narrative and Whitworth stupid. From his briefcase he withdrew a copy of the first RUS letter and handed it to Whitworth. "I believe that you wrote this letter. Did you?"

Whitworth lowered his head and stared at a glass of water. His hand began to shake and rattle the ice in the glass. For about a minute he kept his head lowered and said nothing.

Here was RUS cowering and teetering on the precipice of confession. Peterson judged that only a little psychological pressure would suffice to nudge him over the brink. All he had to do was bend the rules a little.

As it was, he obeyed them and said nothing until Whitworth looked up and stuttered, "I . . . I . . . I don't want to answer that."

"Will you allow us to search your residence?" Peterson asked.

"I think I should talk to someone first."

"Would you be willing to take a polygraph examination?"

"Before I do that, I would like to talk to a lawyer."

"All right, that ends our interview. Since you want to talk to a lawyer, we can't question you anymore. I need to consult the Justice Department in Washington to see what we do next. May I use the phone?" Too traumatized to speak, Whitworth nodded affirmatively.

Peterson called Smits, who was standing by at the Sacramento field office. Keeping the line to Peterson open, Smits in turn called Szady in Washington and asked him to obtain advice from Martin.

While Peterson was on the phone, Whitworth asked McElwee what was likely to happen. "I believe we have grounds for a search warrant," replied McElwee. "We probably will have to secure your residence while we obtain it."

"What do you mean, secure?"

"Your residence will have to be sealed, the contents impounded, guards posted to prevent destruction of evidence."

"Yeah, I see what you mean."

"In any case, you may be arrested. I don't know. We can't arrest you without authority from the Justice Department."

Whitworth blurted, "Why don't you guys just go ahead and search it right now?"

Taking the phone from Peterson, McElwee asked his supervisor, William Mullins, for legal guidance as to whether they could accept Whitworth's consent to a search. Mullins promised to talk to Washington and call back.

While they waited, Whitworth turned on the radio and soon heard a newscaster announce the arrest of John Walker. Quickly switching off the radio, he trembled so that he had to sit down.

No one spoke until Smits telephoned some twenty minutes later with word from Martin. While the guilt of Whitworth was transparent to all, the government lacked adequate evidence to secure an arrest warrant. If Whitworth gave written consent, they could search. But arrest would have to be delayed pending collection of more evidence.

As soon as Whitworth signed the consent form, at 2:38 P.M., McElwee grabbed the floppy disc and letter he had seen Whitworth remove from the computer. The letter was addressed to John Walker. Peterson recognized in it the same style they had discerned in the RUS letters. He thought he also recognized a plain-language code.

When Peterson and McElwee left, they waved to FBI agents parked in front of Whitworth's trailer. The surveillants made no effort to conceal their presence from anybody.

In Norfolk by midafternoon some twenty-five agents congregated around John Walker's house awaiting a search warrant. Walker after his arrest voluntarily had turned over the key and code to the burglar alarm, hoping to avoid the damage of a break-in. But the agents carried crowbars, sledgehammers, x-ray equipment, and magnetic and other detection devices for use inside. They were in no mood to be gentle. Rather, they intended, literally, to tear the place apart in quest of hidden evidence. They also were concerned that Walker, in light of his wild character and now known penchant for exotic weaponry and gadgets, might have booby-trapped the house.

Jerry Richards from the laboratory, who had stayed up all night and through the morning analyzing documents from the Maryland drop, led the search team. Richards is a huge man, six feet six inches tall. When the warrant arrived, he and about fourteen other agents were milling around on the rear deck of the house. Just as an agent opened the front door, the deck collapsed under their weight with a loud bang. Thinking for a second that there had been an explosion, Richards asked himself, "Am I still alive?"

Walker's office and den yielded a trove of papers and documents that reeked of espionage. One find confirmed their initial guesses about the identities of D, K, and S, referred to in the letter from Walker to the KGB that had been recovered at the drop. On one page of a small notebook he had written:

D — Jerry
K — Art
S — Mike

There it was. Jerry Whitworth (D), Arthur Walker (K), and John's son, Michael (S), were all members of his ring.

At headquarters Rod Leffler, on scanning the cache from the Maryland countryside, had exclaimed, "I've never seen anything like this!" Now Richards exclaimed the same words when the searchers in Walker's home came across typewritten instructions titled "The Vienna Procedure." In nearly twenty years of analyzing KGB documents and operational practices, he never had seen such minutely detailed and labyrinthine instructions for a clandestine meeting. They discovered equally complicated instructions enabling Walker to signal for an emergency meeting outside the United States and for emergency exchanges inside.

The most arcane item discovered was perhaps the most sinister and revealing. It looked like a gray metal box about the size of a large cigarette lighter. Opening it, they saw that one side of the interior contained a circular dial ringed by numerals. "What do you think this is, Jerry?" an agent asked.

"I don't know. It's unique. It's handmade," Richards said. But his practiced eye noted some strong clues as to the purpose of the device. "I suspect it measures electrical impulses. The numbers indicate the user is supposed to record them. Yes, it's made to read something . . . maybe crypto rotors. That may be it. It may be designed to read the circuitry of a crypto rotor."

"But most of our machines haven't used rotors for years."

"Obviously, the Sovs made this for him when we did."

The rotor reader, which could divine the workings of old machines, proved that again Barbara Walker was right. John Walker had been in the business for many years, as early as the 1960s. As they continued the search, the proof piled up in mountainous proportions.

Wolfinger got home about eight o'clock that Monday night. He had been working under extreme stress without respite since 4:00 A.M. Sunday. Having smoked incessantly since Sunday afternoon, he forlornly faced the ordeal of quitting all over again. Pouring himself a bourbon and water, he slumped down on a sofa.

From an adjoining room his wife cheerfully called, "Hey, I just saw on television that they caught some big spy up around Washington. Did you have anything to do with that?"

"Yes, I did."

His wife hurried in to question him. Drink unfinished, he had fallen into a deep sleep.

Arthur Walker soon multiplied the evidence. Short, slight, almost completely bald, with big horn-rimmed glasses resting on a large, protuberant nose, his finger yellowed by nicotine, Arthur at age fifty-one looked like a man whom life had passed by. Indeed, any artist commissioned to paint a portrait of the quintessential wimp would welcome him as a model. From the beginning, he endeavored to persuade the FBI he was just that and nothing more. From the beginning, Agent Beverly Andress believed he was more.

She and Special Agent Carroll Deane appeared at his three-bedroom brick home in Virginia Beach about 9:00 A.M. on May 20. Feigning surprise and consternation at his brother's arrest, Arthur volunteered to accompany them to the Norfolk field office for an interview.

Andress was barely twenty-eight years old and had no experience in counterintelligence interrogation. Yet she immediately established the psychological climate every expert interrogator strives to create. By her remarks and questions she communicated to Arthur her superior knowledge, and he could not be sure how far it extended to him. She also made him accept the proposition that his obligation was to please her with his answers.

Arthur more or less told the truth about his past — enlistment in the navy at age nineteen, rise through the ranks to the grade of lieutenant commander, business failures after his retirement in 1973, employment as a low-level engineer with the VSE Corporation, a navy contractor. But he steadfastly denied any awareness of his brother's involvement in espionage, and certainly he himself was never involved.

Andress suggested that a polygraph examination might make everybody more confident of the facts, and Arthur readily agreed. Again she read him his rights and explicitly asked if he wished to confer with a lawyer before undergoing the examination. Not at all, Arthur insisted; he had absolutely nothing to hide and therefore no need of a lawyer.

However, as FBI polygrapher Barry Colvert strapped on

the electrodes, Arthur had some afterthoughts. Come to think of it, during the past six months he had become suspicious of brother John. In fact, he was 95 percent sure that John was doing something illegal. Having thus straightened matters out, he took the lie detector test.

Colvert, considered one of if not the very best interrogator and polygrapher in the FBI, concluded that in response to every important question Arthur had lied or been deceptive.

To Arthur, Agent Andress affected shocked disapproval at such deceit. She had thought Arthur was an officer and a gentleman. A proper lady and serious professional such as herself had no time or respect for liars. She dismissed him, curtly observing that until he could tell the truth, further conversation was pointless.

The next morning when the FBI office opened, Arthur was waiting at the door like a pestiferous puppy eager to be let in. He really wanted to resolve any outstanding issues. He had been reflecting, and now he recalled that once he let John look at a classified document from the VSE Corporation. Again he agreed to take a polygraph test; again it indicated he was lying about all significant questions. Andress recommended that he hire a lawyer.

But Arthur kept coming back unbidden, and gradually Andress peeled away his pretenses and elicited some truth. Arthur admitted that he had given John classified documents knowing that they were destined for the Soviets and that he had accepted a payment of twelve thousand dollars for them. Although advised anew of his rights against self-incrimination, he voluntarily signed a confession.

Asked during yet another polygraph test if he ever had spied for the Soviets while in the navy, Arthur said no. The test showed he was lying. But for legal purposes, the signed confession was enough.

Throughout the interviews and polygraph examinations Arthur chain-smoked. Colvert later declared to colleagues that he intended to put the suit he had worn during the examinations in quarantine. "I'm sure it has cancer."

Aboard the carrier *Nimitz,* moored in Haifa harbor, they ushered Seaman Michael Walker into a wardroom. He stood barely five feet six inches tall, weighed 110 pounds, and had the cherubic face of a choirboy; though he was twenty-three, he looked fifteen.

Keith Hitt introduced himself as an agent of the Naval Investigative Service from Rome. "Michael, your father has been arrested on charges of espionage," Hitt began. "He was trying to deliver classified documents from the *Nimitz* to the Soviets. The FBI also found a large number of documents from the *Nimitz* in your father's home. We believe you gave those documents to your father. Next to your bunk we found a stack of classified documents nearly two feet high. We found many more documents in the fan room next to your office. We think you put them there. Now Michael, I would like to talk to you. But you do not *have* to talk to me."

Hitt then formally advised Michael of the same rights to counsel and silence that a civilian enjoys. Pale and frightened, Michael said he did not want to talk.

"I understand; that's perfectly all right," Hitt calmly replied. "I will be aboard for some time. If you change your mind, let me know."

A couple of hours later, word came from the brig that Michael wanted to see Hitt. Tears welling in his eyes, he said, "It's true," and began to confess. Hitt interrupted him and summoned a lawyer, who restated the rights against self-incrimination and asked Michael if he wanted to consult a lawyer.

Michael said no, he wanted to tell the truth, and he thereupon poured out a confession. Since 1983 he had been providing his father with secret navy documents and messages. He had stolen hundreds of them, so many that he could not give an exact count. His father had paid him one thousand dollars but promised much more.

"Is that why you did it, for the money?" Hitt asked.

"I guess I did it for my father."

Manacled and escorted by Hitt, Michael was flown from Haifa to Andrews Air Force Base outside Washington, then arraigned in Baltimore on espionage charges.

That Friday night, May 24, Michael's pretty twenty-one-year-old wife, Rachel, drove five hours from Norfolk to Baltimore. She lost herself in a dangerous part of the city and in tears called the FBI office for directions. David Major, the agent in charge of counterintelligence in Baltimore, sent an agent to bring her to the office.

At the sight of her, Michael sobbed, "I'm in real trouble."

She wrapped her arms around him and said, "Honey, we will find some way out."

"No, not this time. I'm in real trouble. There's no way out."

Major asked Rachel if she had reserved a room for the night. She replied that she intended to drive back to Norfolk.

"You can't do that," Major said. "It's almost midnight, and you're in no condition to drive."

"I don't have any money for a room."

Major gave her fifty dollars of his own money, called a motel, then telephoned her father in Norfolk to tell him of the arrangements. "Thank you, Mr. Major," he said. "I guarantee you will get your money back." Rachel's father, a retired enlisted man, had been proud that his daughter married the son of an officer. Now he added, "I'm really ashamed. I'm very sorry, Mr. Major."

7

Reconstructing
a Disaster

THE ARRESTS of John, Michael, and Arthur Walker; the
spectacle of father, son, and brother uniting in treason;
the pathos of a mother unwittingly sending her son
to prison; the revelation that a spy ring had survived undetected in the United States for at least seventeen years —
all combined to inspire worldwide headlines and innumerable
stories.

The fact that both John and Arthur Walker had served on
submarines during much of their naval careers caused many
to conclude that the greatest damage they did was to American submarine forces. Press accounts speculated that perhaps
they even had imperiled the U.S. strategic triad of bombers,
land-based missiles, and submarine missiles.

Amid all the publicity about the Walkers and their families,
scant attention was paid to Jerry Whitworth. But early on,
John Martin and FBI analysts recognized what most people
fail to realize even today: of the conspirators identified in the
Walker spy ring, Jerry Whitworth during the latter years was
by far the most important, and he demanded the most urgent
attention.

John Walker's letter to the KGB retrieved from the Maryland drop and materials found in his home strongly supported an earlier hypothesis: Before retiring from the navy in 1976, Walker doubtless purveyed to the Soviets secrets to which he personally had access, and he had access to many priceless data. But since 1976 Walker had acted as a principal agent, delivering to the KGB secrets supplied to him by subsources. As spymaster, he was indispensable to the functioning of the ring. However, for the past nine years he by himself probably had been able to steal little of value. He was dependent upon others, and to gauge the losses inflicted by the ring, one had to look to the others.

Arthur Walker very well may have given the Soviets secrets before he left the navy in 1973, and he admitted pilfering classified documents from his civilian employer. Yet, as John Walker noted in his status report to the KGB, Arthur's access was comparatively narrow and limited.

The navy feared that the hundreds of documents stolen by Michael Walker constituted a grave loss. Michael, though, was an ordinary young seaman without a Top Secret clearance, and his reach did not extend into the navy's most secret sanctums. His confession fairly well defined the boundaries of his treason. With time, the damage he did could be assessed with reasonable accuracy and repairs initiated, albeit at great cost.

Jerry Whitworth was the one known member of the ring who in recent years could have inflicted irreparable and potentially mortal damage on the country. During his last five tours in the navy, he had access to most of its ultrasecret cryptographic and communications data. Writing as RUS, Whitworth stated that he had transmitted cryptographic key material, technical manuals for cipher machines, and intelligence messages to the Soviets. How long did he do that? Which keys? Which manuals? Did he spy continuously or sporadically? Did he give the Soviets just enough to keep them interested, or did he give them everything within his grasp? Had messages he passed been transmitted by the same cipher machines and keys he betrayed? The nation desperately needed to know the answers.

There was another immediate and compelling reason requiring comprehensive investigation of Whitworth, the reconstruction of his whole life, the gathering of every available detail about his service in the navy, his behavior, movements, and income. For purposes of damage assessment, investigators and analysts would expend tens of thousands of manhours peering into the pasts of John, Arthur, and Michael Walker. But for purposes of prosecution, the government needed no more evidence against them. The scrupulously obtained confessions of Arthur and Michael ensured their convictions. The case against John Walker, consisting of materials secured from the drop and his home, together with the signed statements of his own son and brother, was overwhelming.

By contrast, the legal case against Whitworth at the time was thin. Although everyone now was sure he wrote the RUS letters, there was no proof, and without proof, the letters probably would be inadmissible as evidence. John Walker's notebook indicated that D stood for Jerry; his letter to the KGB indicated that D had collaborated in the past and predicted he would resume his cooperation. Yet Walker's letter, standing by itself, was inadmissible hearsay. The excerpts of letters Walker left at the drop undoubtedly were written by Whitworth; Whitworth and Walker undeniably were friends or associates of long standing. Even assuming that all this could be admitted into evidence, an able defense attorney would still ask, So what? John Walker was a demonstrable liar, a traitor who had betrayed everybody and everything. Jerry

Whitworth, with twenty-one years of exemplary service to his country, scarcely could be blamed because he also had been betrayed. And how could anyone place credence in anything a fellow so scurvy as John Walker had written?

While existing evidence justified the arrest of Whitworth, without much more evidence his conviction would be doubtful, maybe even unlikely. The question of who would be entrusted to develop and prosecute the case against Whitworth thus was crucial. So was the question of which U.S. attorney's office and FBI field office would be primarily responsible for amassing the evidence.

Without hesitation, Martin said to Dion, "It has to be Buck, Leida, and the Count."

William "Buck" Farmer and Leida Schoggen were assistant U.S. attorneys charged with special prosecutions in San Francisco. John Martin had come to know them well during the time Farmer handled the sensitive espionage case of James Durward Harper. They formed an exceptional legal team with an unusual past.

The son of a banker, Farmer spent his childhood in small towns of Kentucky, Tennessee, and Alabama. He entered Princeton University with the intention of becoming a Marine Corps officer, then devoting his career to some form of public service. During college summers he trained in the Marine Platoon Leader Corps, which offered him the option of accepting a commission upon graduation.

Princeton maintained a program whereby distinguished alumni counseled students about their careers, and Farmer's counselor was Allen Dulles, the director of the CIA. Dulles persuaded him that he could broaden his choices in government and better prepare himself to serve by studying law rather than joining the marines. A faculty adviser suggested that he would benefit from studying in a completely different part of the country and recommended, among other institutions, the University of Texas Law School.

After finishing at Texas, Farmer went to work for the Federal Trade Commission in Washington, believing that he could further free enterprise by combating monopolistic practices. He enjoyed the work, but when his youthful marriage disintegrated he wanted to escape Washington and unhappy memories. An assignment took him for the first time to San Francisco, and he rode a cable car to Russian Hill. There he looked down on the magnificent city surrounded by bays and green hills in the distance. The air was crisp and pure, the sunshine brighter than he could remember, and the pastels of the buildings below reminded him of the south of France and Italy. He said to himself, "Here is where I want to spend the rest of my life."

Transferred to San Francisco, Farmer became the second attorney on a complex antitrust case brought years before by the government against a petroleum company. New people in Washington reviewing the case were contemptuous of those who filed it, declaring there was only one chance in twenty of winning. Just as the trial was approaching its climax, two weeks before closing arguments, the lead government attorney fell seriously ill and Farmer had to take over. To the astonishment of the Justice Department and the expensive battery of defense attorneys alike, the government won the case.

In preparing antitrust litigation, Farmer had to investigate and collect evidence himself. The experience taught him to build complicated cases from obscure records, but it also limited his trial work, which is what he liked most. For the fun of it, he volunteered to assist the Criminal Division when it needed an extra prosecutor. Soon he was invited to join the Criminal Division full time. He accepted even though he had

John Walker (with toupee)

Arthur Walker (with toupee)

Michael Walker

Jerry Whitworth

Above: John Walker's record of payments to Whitworth.

Below: A note from Whitworth to John Walker. It reads:

Still have

I got *all* "S" [Secret] & above
& important "C" [Confidential] GENSERV [General Service]
TFC [traffic] of the 12 mos.

Pics of new device—roll dispenser

Includes flag   Battle force Cdr. [Commander]

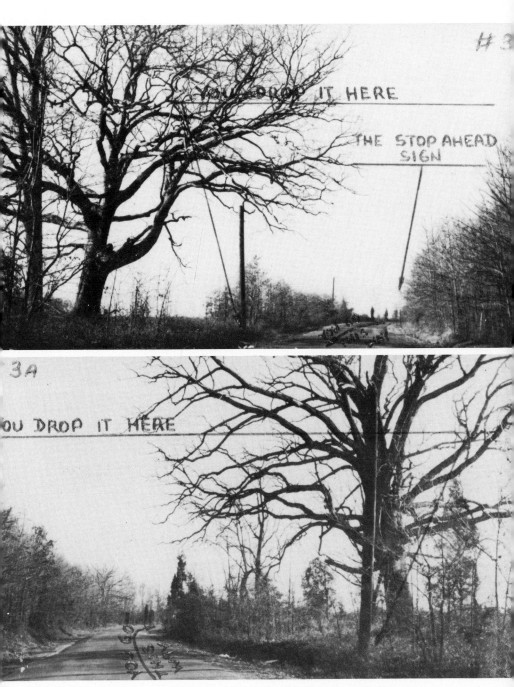

KGB pictures of drop sites for classified material. When the trees and bushes were
in leaf, the sites were sometimes hard to identify from such snapshots.

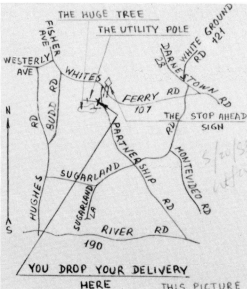

THE HUGE TREE
THE UTILITY POLE
WHITE GROUND RD 121
DARNESTOWN RD 28
WESTERLY AVE
FISHER AVE
WHITES
FERRY RD 107
BUDD RD
GUDD RD
N ↑ S
THE STOP AHEAD SIGN
PARTNERSHIP
MONTEVIDEO RD
RD
SUGARLAND RD
SUGARLAND LA
HUGHES
RIVER RD 190

YOU DROP YOUR DELIVERY HERE

DROP YOUR DELIVERY BEHIND A UTILITY POLE ON PARTNERSHIP RD NEAR ITS INTERSECTION WITH WHITES FERRY RD (107).

THE UTILITY POLE IN QUESTION IS LOCATED AT A HUGE TREE ON THE RIGHT HAND SIDE OF PARTNERSHIP RD ABOUT 0.1 MILE FROM THE INTERSECTION OF PARTNERSHIP RD AND WHITES FERRY RD (YOUR DROP POINT WILL BE ON YOUR RIGHT WHEN YOU DRIVE ON PARTNERSHIP RD FROM WHITES FERRY RD TOWARD SUGARLAND RD).

BEFORE REACHING YOUR DROP POINT YOU'LL PASS A ROAD SIGN "STOP AHEAD" ON YOUR LEFT. GOING SOUTH YOU'LL SEE THE REVERSE SIDE OF THAT SIGN THUS YOUR DROP POINT IS LOCATED BETWEEN THE HUGE TREE ON YOUR RIGHT AND THE STOP AHEAD SIGN ON YOUR LEFT.

(PHOTOS # 3, 3A, 3B, 3C)

THIS PICTURE IS IN THE DIRECTION OF WHITES FERRY RD (1

THIS IS A CLOSE-UP VIEW OF YOUR DROP POINT FROM THE OPPOSITE DIRECTION.
THIS PICTURE IS IN THE DIRECTION OF SUGARLAND RD.
THAT IS WHAT YOU SEE GOING ON PARTNERSHIP RD FROM WHITES FERRY RD TOWARD SUGARLAND RD.

KGB instructions about drops, for John Walker.

The trash bag and contents recovered by the FBI from John Walker's last drop. Pages at bottom left are the "Dear Friend" letter from Walker to his Soviet case officer. At right are pages from a Whitworth letter to Walker.

John Walker reenacts copying secret documents with a Minox camera.

Jerry Whitworth; his wife, "the lady in red"; and the Rolls-Royce hired when the USS *Enterprise* arrived in home port in 1983.

John Walker in KKK robes, which he donned in
one of his many flamboyant poses as a private
detective.

A sophisticated device manufactured in KGB laboratories in Moscow and found
in John Walker's house by the FBI. Its purpose is to divine circuitry and settings
on American cipher machines.

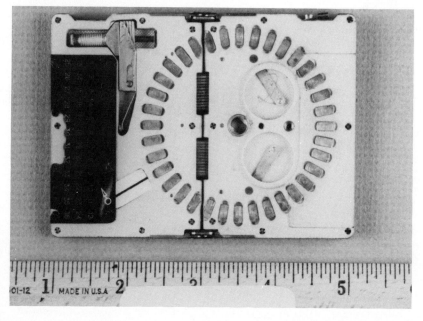

William Farmer (left) with FBI agent John Peterson during their investigation aboard the USS *Enterprise*.

been named assistant chief of the Antitrust Division, staffed by twenty attorneys.

There he began to put away drug traffickers, including three major Colombian heroin kings. One afternoon in 1982 Farmer received a collect telephone call from an inmate at Lompoc Prison.

"Mr. Farmer, they's gonna kill you. They's gonna kill your kids, too. Now, don't hang up, Mr. Farmer. You don't know me, but I know about you. You have two boys, right?"

"Yes."

"A few weeks ago you was gonna take those boys camping in Wyoming, right?"

"Yes."

"But you didn't go. At the last minute, for some reason, you didn't go, right?"

"That's right."

"Well, that was a good thing, because they planned to kill all three of you. It was all set. Now they want me to kill you. But I ain't no killer, Mr. Farmer. I need to talk to you."

The caller turned out to be Leon "Magic" Colburn, a bank robber and burglar of some repute who was about to be paroled. Working in the print shop where a prison newspaper was published, Magic saw a story about a Mafia hit man. Magic as a joke inserted his own picture with the article, and upon its publication, prison inmates concluded that he really was somebody, a big-time assassin. Cocaine dealer José Robert Gomez-Soto approached him, confided his determination to avenge himself, and offered Magic a huge sum of money and cocaine to kill Farmer once Magic was out of prison.

Authorities promptly brought him to San Francisco and Farmer. "I'm just a pussycat, Mr. Farmer. Banks, a store now and then, okay. But I don't believe in drugs and killin', least of all killin' kids."

With the help of Magic, Gomez-Soto again was prosecuted. The judge sentenced him and his son to life imprisonment for conspiracy to murder a federal official. Later, however, Interpol informed Farmer that a Colombian cocaine cabal was plotting another assassination attempt against him and a witness.

From the time Farmer realized that he indeed was the target of a serious, well-conceived assassination plot, he resolved not to be intimidated personally nor deterred professionally. He would comport himself prudently, carry a weapon, heed reasonable security advice. But he would not shrink or hide or paralyze himself with fright.

Now and then at night the sounds of branches rustling against the roof or the wind rattling a window awakened him. Sure that the Colombians had finally come, he would roll off the bed and, revolver in hand, crouch in the darkness, waiting, sometimes for as long as an hour. But he never ran away.

Trained by the marines to keep fit through rigorous physical exercise, he regularly jogged, swam, and worked out on Nautilus machines at the downtown Olympic Club. His physique together with strong, even facial features, fair complexion, happy blue eyes, and luxuriant brown hair made him very attractive to women.

One morning as he combed his hair, a large swath fell out. He touched his head and another patch came off, painlessly, as if it had no roots. In disbelief, he patted the back of his head and more hair fell. Stroking his forearm, he brushed the hairs off as easily as if they were snowflakes.

A physician advised that he was suffering from alopecia areata, a condition that often results in the complete loss of all body hair, even eyebrows and eyelashes. While on a small percentage of victims hair eventually may reappear just as mysteriously as it vanished, there is no medical cure or treatment for the malady. Neither is the cause known. But acute, sudden stress has precipitated the affliction in many cases.

118

Doctors who treated Farmer suspected that he had so totally repressed his fear, so rigidly contained it within himself, that it could find no natural outlet. Probably it ultimately vented itself in the form of alopecia areata.

As he daily assumed what to him was the extraterrestrial countenance of a cartoon character from another planet, Farmer thought, "I'm going to be a freak, a leper. I will be offensive to everybody. No girl will ever have anything to do with me."

At the time, Leida Schoggen was an assistant U.S. attorney in the San Jose office, respected for her native intelligence and professional competence. The FBI, Internal Revenue Service, and police delighted in working with her because of her quick comprehension of their problems and willingness to help with them. Provoked by indolence or stupidity, Leida, as everyone called her, occasionally indulged in an outburst of profanity. She never spoke harshly, though, to subordinates. And she had been known to take a frightened young black secretary to lunch on her first day at work and to stay late with others to coach them on office procedures.

Invariably, when business took her to the San Francisco office, the word spread, "Leida is here." Men found pretexts to step into the corridors in hope of catching sight of her coming or going. She was tall and wore her hair in a pageboy that framed lovely hazel-green eyes, a straight nose, and a wide mouth, which often broke into an even broader smile. John Martin considered her both the most appealing woman and one of the best lawyers in the entire Justice Department, and his opinion was not unique.

Leida and Farmer scarcely knew each other. But when the San Francisco and San Jose staffs assembled for their annual party, she sat down beside him and, without mentioning his loss of hair, endeavored to console him. He asked about her past, and she answered frankly.

Her father, a psychologist, was a university professor, and during her childhood they lived in Kansas, Oregon, and England. At Grinnell College in Iowa, through a close black friend, she became interested in minority concerns and problems. After college she went to Chicago, where she lived and taught school in a black ghetto. There she also met and married a policeman, but the marriage failed. At the same time, she came to doubt the value of her teaching, and so she left for law school. Having seen how crime ravages the downtrodden especially, she gravitated into government service in hope of doing something to curtail it.

In turn, Farmer briefly summarized his own background, concluding, "I never expected to wind up a freak."

"I always thought you were the most handsome man in San Francisco. I still think you are."

Leida Schoggen and Buck Farmer became friends, then passionate lovers and professional partners, sharing the same values, ideals, and ambition to serve. Sometimes in the evening, on leaving a restaurant, they behaved like teenagers, embracing and kissing on the street. After Leida transferred to San Francisco, they helped each other on cases, and they found that the legal talents of one complemented those of the other.

Almost from the moment Bill Smits first briefed them about Whitworth, pressure upon Farmer and Schoggen to arrest Whitworth mounted. In Washington an FBI spokesman imprudently indicated to reporters that more arrests would follow that of John Walker and he specifically referred to "a California man." Learning of this, Whitworth understood who the "California man" was and thereby precluded any further FBI efforts to question him. Members of Congress, already enraged by the Walker case, demanded to know why the FBI did not arrest the remaining spies, if in fact there were more. And the twenty-four-hour surveillance of Whitworth initiated to prevent his flight could not be sustained indefinitely.

In accordance with Martin's advice, Farmer informed Whitworth's attorney that the government intended to arrest him. He suggested that Whitworth might prefer to surrender voluntarily at the Federal Building in San Francisco rather than suffer the indignity of being arrested, handcuffed, and dragged away from his home in the sight of his neighbors. On Monday, June 3, 1985, Whitworth, bracketed fore and aft by FBI surveillants, drove from Davis and gave himself up. He thereby placed his case under San Francisco jurisdiction, just as Martin planned.

In jail, Whitworth engaged a new lawyer, James L. Larson, and adopted a pose of defiant and aggrieved innocence. Long an inveterate letter-writer, he drafted dozens of appeals to friends or acquaintances soliciting their support. One recipient, who, like Whitworth, had served as a communications supervisor on the carrier *Enterprise,* replied:

When they showed you in chains that Monday night on the news and the subsequent spot reports, my first reaction was total disbelief; almost speechless; unable to understand what was going on. Secondary reactions were outrage that built with each newscast. Walker's comment, "I feel like a celebrity," pissed me off to no end. That asshole better grow the fuck up.

Then I had many thoughts re you selling us all down the river. Were those ball-bustin' years on the *Enterprise* down the toilet? The efforts of all those people in vain? Did you sell me down the river? I asked you on the fone if you had anything to do with this — you said "NO." That NO rings in my head, Jerry. I'm having a lot of trouble believing it. I'm trying my damnest to understand and see through all the media hype and believe this guy I shared many rare moments with was just a victim of circumstances. If I was never an RM [radioman], I guess my viewpoint would be different, but knowing what's at stake and the severity of all this biases the way I see it.

The investigation of Whitworth proceeded on three fronts simultaneously. Agents of the FBI and Naval Investigative Service began interviewing navy personnel and civilians who had known him at various stages of his life and career. Ultimately, hundreds of people would be questioned. Farmer, Schoggen, and John Dion, dispatched from Washington to help, personally talked to many sources. For some of the interviews, they flew to Pearl Harbor and onto the *Enterprise* at sea. Gradually, from the information gathered by the FBI, the NIS, and their own interviews, the prosecutors pieced together a detailed biography and psychological portrait of their adversary, the traitor who dominated their thoughts seven days a week.

Jerry Alfred Whitworth was born in Muldrow, Oklahoma, a rural town of some three thousand people near the Arkansas border. His parents separated about the time of his birth, and he never really knew his father. When he was eight, his mother married a man who apparently disliked him. He lived mostly with his grandparents and on an uncle's farm, where he helped raise soybeans and vegetables. In high school he was an indifferent student who majored in vocational agriculture. A skinny, affable country boy, he was average in every way. The only distinguishing characterization of him appeared in a 1957 senior class yearbook, which referred to him as "the class clown."

In the memories of men who had associated with him twenty to twenty-five years before, during his first years in the navy, Whitworth was little more than a hazy blur. And from navy records, his early career appeared quite ordinary.

After attending boot camp in 1957, he served aboard the

aircraft carrier *Bon Homme Richard* as a storekeeper, a kind of supply clerk, and his performance was average. At the end of his enlistment, in 1960, he enrolled in a small California junior college; he did very poorly there. Having failed a number of courses, he reenlisted in the navy in late 1962 and again was a storekeeper, at a California shore station. In return for his commitment to serve at least six more years, the navy in 1965 sent him to its basic six-month course for radiomen. Beginning in May 1967, he attended the advanced nine-month course for radiomen, then a five-week course in computer systems. These superb schools qualified him to operate and repair the most sophisticated communications and cryptographic equipment.

In 1968 and 1969, during some of the fiercest fighting of the Vietnam War, he was in the Gulf of Tonkin aboard a communications relay ship that forwarded messages to and from U.S. combat forces. After a year on the aircraft carrier *Ranger,* he went as an instructor to the Naval Training Center in San Diego, where he met John Walker.

While in San Diego in 1971, he also met a sixteen-year-old girl, Brenda Reis, who had won a trip to California in a science contest back in her native North Dakota. Although Whitworth was almost thirty-two, he struck up a relationship that later culminated in their marriage.

From pleasant duty in beautiful San Diego, Whitworth went to a Spartan outpost, Diego Garcia, a small, barren atoll in the middle of the Indian Ocean. The United States had just begun to develop the atoll as a communications base to support fleet operations in the Indian Ocean and Middle East, and conditions were primitive. There being almost nothing on which to spend his pay, Whitworth saved most of it. When his tour on Diego Garcia ended in May 1974, he left the navy and settled in San Diego.

The decision later puzzled Farmer and Schoggen. What had

he proposed to do? His accumulated service years were too few to entitle him to a pension. He had tried night school in San Diego and failed. He had no civilian profession or vocation. Nobody figured out what he did between June and December 1974 except learn to fly and try to make money by spotting swordfish in the Gulf of California, a typically absurd Whitworth enterprise. Regardless, in December he returned to the navy and on Christmas Eve reported to Fort Monmouth, New Jersey, to begin a special course in satellite communications.

His next action was even more surprising. He volunteered for another tour on Diego Garcia, the forlorn atoll he had left the preceding May. Why? It wasn't as if he was returning to be near a girlfriend; there were no females within hundreds of miles. Nor was he seeking cultural enrichment from storied cities or great museums and galleries. There was nothing on or near Diego Garcia. It made no sense.

As Farmer and Schoggen studied the records and interviews with people who had known Whitworth during his last ten years or so in the navy, they discerned other curious developments.

Whitworth always had been an adequate sailor, and up until 1974 he was a good if not spectacular radioman. But beginning with his second posting to Diego Garcia in February 1975 and at every subsequent duty station, his performance was positively outstanding. Farmer and Schoggen consulted one of the navy's most distinguished enlisted men, Master Chief Thomas Francis Bennett, himself a radioman who had served in some of the same types of billets as Whitworth. Reviewing Whitworth's record, Bennett concluded that from Diego Garcia on, he had been "darn near a 4.0 sailor."

"What's a 4.0 sailor?" Schoggen asked.

"He's a guy who walks on water without getting his shoes wet."

How did he suddenly become so outstanding? In other interviews, Farmer and Schoggen received various answers. But in the main, his excellence seemed to derive from wholehearted dedication to duty, punctilious adherence to regulations, and a willingness to absorb himself in details that bored others. People remembered that he usually was on the job before anyone else and that he often remained after everybody else left. At sea, while others watched the evening movie, he would stay sealed in his office, studying. Whereas other petty officers would assign subordinates to photocopy documents or destroy used key material, he often would attend to these mundane chores himself. He was interested in all matters pertaining to communications, cryptography, and secret message traffic, matters large and small, even those outside the purview of his normal responsibilities. Everyone attributed his work habits and interests to a commendable determination to grow professionally.

Farmer and Schoggen saw another difference. To men who knew Whitworth during his first fifteen years in the navy, he was a faceless fringe figure. Nobody could provide a fix on him. But many of those who served with him after 1974 had definite recollections of him. And in the eyes of many, he appeared to be an intellectual and a worldly sophisticate.

He ostentatiously read the *Wall Street Journal* and guides to financial investment while boasting of his success in the stock market. He talked endlessly and, to fellow sailors, incomprehensibly about the philosophy of libertarianism. He would have everybody believe that he was a gourmet cook and an informed lover of classical music. He sprinkled his speech with polysyllabic malapropisms. As if to emphasize his worldliness, he let be known that he was an atheist. And in an apparent effort to convey his superiority, he treated underlings with aloofness, arrogance, and condescension.

As Farmer and Schoggen suspected and ultimately confirmed, all this was sham. The supposedly astute investor idiotically bought Krugerrands, coins from the Franklin mint, and worthless futures that cost him ten thousand dollars. He had no real grasp of libertarianism or any other political philosophy, and some schoolteachers who had sailed with him laughed at his intellectual airs, which to them were embarrassingly empty. His idea of a gourmet meal was spicy Indian curry at a second-rate restaurant.

A letter Whitworth wrote on February 28, 1980, to Senate Majority Leader Robert Byrd mirrored his actual intellect and erudition. It said:

> Dear Sir:
> I am a chief petty officer in the USN stationed at NTCC, NAS Alameda, CA. I am making more money now than I would have believed possible 15 years ago. But there is a problem, INFLATION.
> Inflation is going to destroy our great country. What does our leaders (!) do, keep on spending more than it takes in [sic]. The amount going into the government coffer has been going up dramatically at [sic] you (U.S. Congress) spend even more!
> Frankly, you and your colleagues have lost my respect. I no longer see you as leaders but selfish individuals, looking out for your narrow self-interest and that of the special interest groups that meet your short-term goals.
> What will history have to say, I wonder.
> Sincerely,
> Jerry A. Whitworth

There was yet another difference between the first and second stages of Whitworth's naval career. During the first, he had no — or at least relatively limited — access to the most critical communications and cryptographic secrets. During the second, he enjoyed virtually unlimited access. In fact, had someone set out to position himself in sensitive billets, he scarcely would have done better than Whitworth did, whether by design or happenstance. A succinct navy summary of his post-1974 assignments and duties told a portentous story to all who understood naval jargon:

08 Mar 75–28 Mar 76
Naval Communications Station, Diego Garcia, RM1/TS Clearance
Leading Petty Officer in charge of the Technical Control Facility; was Communications Security Control Systems (CMS) Custodian.

12 Jun 76–05 Jul 78
USS *Constellation* (CV-64), RM1/TS Clearance
Facilities Control Supervisor. Responsible for the operation and maintenance of all UHF and HF radio circuits during under-way operations. Controls selection of transmitting, receiving and terminal equipment; use of cryptographic equipment including shifts and adjustments.
RMC/TS Clearance
Facilities Control Work Center Supervisor. Communications Watch Officer. Sealed Authentication System (SAS) team member. Communication Command Duty Officer.

10 Aug 78–10 Aug 79
USS *Niagara Falls* (AFS-3), RMC/TS Clearance
Radio Chief Petty Officer. CMS Custodian. Task Group Communications Operator.

10 Sep 79–Oct 82
Naval Telecommunications Center (NTCC), Alameda NAS, RMC/RMCS/TS Clearance
Administrations Chief and Message Center Chief. CMS Custodian and Assistant Officer in Charge.

01 Dec 80–15 Mar 81
Naval Communications Station, Stockton, CA, RMC/TS Clearance
Temporary Additional Duty to Stockton as Leading Petty Of-

ficer in charge of Tech Control. Complete access to Comm Center, with exception of CMS.

11 Oct 82–31 Oct 83
USS *Enterprise* (CVN-65), RMC/TS Clearance
  Tech Control Chief. Supervision of maintenance and operation of communications equipment. Access to crypto material pertaining to limited RS material SPECAT, TICON or any message with special handling caveats. Full access to secret cryptographic key cards and the safes where they were stored. Cryptographic equipment to include the KWR-37s, KG-14s, KG-36s, KW-7s, KY-3s and KY-57s. In making the telephone patches for external communications, 50 covered or uncovered communications lines would be available with the capability of monitoring any of the voice circuits involved.

In one of the most fortunate acts in its whole conduct of the case, the navy assigned James Alsup, a young lieutenant from the Judge Advocate General's Corps, to assist the prosecution. Alsup had attended law school after four years in the navy as an enlisted man. Upon graduation, he could have easily stepped into a lucrative law practice with his father or brother back in New Mexico. He felt, though, that he owed something to the navy, which had helped finance his education. So he accepted a commission and contracted to serve four years.

At the end of his obligated service, in December 1985, he would either have to leave the navy or commit himself to several more years in it. His brother, who recently had reaped a contingency fee of $600,000, was importuning him to leave for private practice. His wife, Mary Jane, had just given birth to a son, of whom they were boundlessly proud. Living costs in the San Francisco area are high, and on a lieutenant's pay the Alsups were hard-pressed.

During the first of the preliminary proceedings, Alsup, tall, ramrod straight, his short dark hair neatly trimmed, stood in uniform in the stately paneled chamber where Whitworth would be tried. He heard Farmer say, "Your Honor, for the United States, William S. Farmer, Jr., Leida Schoggen, Lieutenant James Alsup, United States Navy. . . ."

As an enlisted man, Alsup had worked in ultrasecret communications and cryptanalysis. The moment he saw Whitworth's service record, he knew, just as Bill Smits and John Peterson knew after the RUS letters in 1984. The words *for the United States* echoed in his thoughts. That night, with the concurrence of his wife, he resolved to remain in the navy for the duration of the trial and beyond, no matter what the cost.

Referring to the summary of Whitworth's assignments and duties, Farmer asked Alsup what it all meant. The lieutenant, who regarded both Farmer and Schoggen as he would military superiors, reflected and composed his answer carefully. "It means that there are no cryptographic or communications data of any importance to which he did not have access. It means that if he gave them everything he could have given them, there is nothing of importance about the U.S. Navy they do not know. That is the minimum meaning. Personally, I'm afraid it means much more."

Meanwhile, Smits, Peterson, Griego, Dion, Farmer, and Schoggen had begun efforts to track Whitworth through the copious notes and records confiscated from John Walker's home. Copies arrived from Wolfinger in Norfolk in early June, and they all crammed themselves into Smits's office to sort them out.

As they passed records around, John Dion meditated upon two sheets of paper inscribed with Delphic notations. After a while, he handed one to Leida Schoggen and asked, "What does this look like to you?"

She saw three lines of typed capital letters. Imprinted on

the first line were the letters *J F M A M J J A S O N D;* then
a repetition of the same letters, with the number *76* typed
above the first *J;* then another repetition, with the number *77*
above the first *J.* Handwritten below each letter was a number, a *1* or *2.* Drawn below the numbers were brackets and
below them subtotals of the numbers enclosed and some specific dates. A second and third line were typed in the same
style, though the handwritten notations were different. Leida
said, "It looks like some sort of a calendar."

"It is. The letters obviously stand for months, the numerals
above for years. But you know what I think this really is? I
think it's a pay record."

All the handwritten notations on the second sheet paralleled those on the first except that they covered only the period from 1975 through 1979. They also provided a little more
information. Above the date 8/77 were the letters *HK;* above
the dates 11/77 and 2/78 the letters *SD.*

Dion had made a profound discovery that proved to be the
most important and revealing of the Walker-Whitworth case.
The two sheets did constitute a record of payments from
Walker to Whitworth, and this record became the key that
unlocked the ring.

As Smits pointed out, it also answered, immediately and
grimly, a fundamental question that had stared at them ever
since receipt of the first RUS letter. "The first payment — I'm
sure the four means four thousand dollars — was made in
either January, February, or March 1975. Recall that Barbara
said Whitworth came to see Walker in Norfolk in February
1975. He had just finished the satellite communications school
in New Jersey and was on his way back to Diego Garcia. Now
we know why. The payment either was for something from
the school or a retainer. It doesn't matter. Obviously, as early
as February 1975 Whitworth was a spy."

Smits pointed out something else. "Look on the third line

at the notation '100 dash June 80.' That means that in June 1980 Walker paid Whitworth one hundred thousand dollars. It's unheard of. The KGB never would pay that kind of money to anybody, much less a navy enlisted man, unless he was doing something fantastic."

Among the mass of documents, papers, and notes taken from John Walker's home were three passports documenting foreign travels from 1973 to 1985; calendars for most of those same years annotated with abbreviations such as *F/F* and *Exch.*; credit card, hotel, and travel receipts; and the inordinately detailed Soviet instructions for face-to-face meetings (F/F) and drops, or exchanges (Exch.), as the KGB termed them. Walker's retaining the instructions perhaps was understandable; they were so complicated that no one could confidently commit them to memory. His keeping all the other data was incomprehensible. Yet here they were, and the FBI made the most of them.

Working eighteen hours a day in bursts of up to ten hours straight, Smits entered the dates and other information from the pay record into his computer. He then endeavored to enter dates and information from Walker's records that matched or seemed relevant to those on the pay record.

For example, Walker's travel records revealed that on August 10, 1977, he landed in Hong Kong. On Smits's computer screen, this date showed up in a box containing the notation from the pay record "HK 8/77." With help from the navy, Smits filled the box with other entries: USS *Constellation* in Hong Kong August 10–15, 1977; Whitworth takes leave from *Constellation* in Hong Kong August 11, 1977. From Walker's passport and annotated calendar, Smits added more entries to the same box: Walker departs Hong Kong August 12; arrives Casablanca August 16; has F/F with KGB in Casablanca August 17.

Another computer box began with the pay record entry

"SD 2/78." By the same methodology, Smits filled it with more entries: January 21, 1978, Walker has F/F with KGB in Vienna; February 14, 1978, Walker arrives by private plane in San Diego; February 14, 1978, USS *Constellation* in port, San Diego; March 11, 1978, Walker effects exchange with KGB, Washington area.

By June 9, 1985, Smits's computer graphics brilliantly illuminated the past in stunning detail. They documented twenty-two meetings between Walker and Whitworth between 1975 and 1984 and a total of $332,000 in payments to Whitworth. They also delineated a clear pattern of operations. Always before servicing a drop or meeting the KGB personally, Walker rendezvoused with Whitworth. After each contact with the KGB, Walker again met Whitworth fairly soon. As in Hong Kong, where Walker arrived on August 10 and departed on August 12, their encounters always were brief, never lasting more than a day or so. Manifestly, they were not social engagements.

The import of the pattern was unmistakable. Walker would receive data from Whitworth, deliver it to the KGB either in the United States or abroad, then personally pay Whitworth as soon as practicable.

On June 11, 1985, Wolfinger flashed to San Francisco and Szady in Washington a superb analysis of Walker's travels since 1975, prepared jointly by the Norfolk office and the headquarters Analytical Unit. Their findings conformed almost perfectly with those of Smits.

Farmer and Schoggen now began to receive evidence from a third source, the Internal Revenue Service. Ever since his days in antitrust work, Farmer had respected the capabilities of IRS criminal investigators, and so did Smits. In San Francisco the IRS had one of its best, Alex Seddio, an ebullient, indefatigable Sicilian dubbed the Tasmanian Devil because of the ferocity with which he pursued criminals. Having been a cryptographer in the Marine Corps, Seddio grasped the meaning and potential consequences of Whitworth's treason. To Farmer he remarked, "You know, when I'm investigating someone, I get to know him, and always when we close in, I feel sorry for him because he's a fellow human being. I'm sorry he's done what he's done and that I have to hurt him. But for Whitworth I feel no pity."

Seddio formed a superb team consisting of Barron Fong, Floyd Hobbs, Florence Poon, and Shannon Hodges. Fong was a tall, slender, quiet special agent with a gift for organization and a love of computers. He could discern meaning in a seemingly mundane personal check or gasoline receipt. Hobbs was a veteran accounting expert who at times worked eighteen hours a day seven days a week. He could distill thousands of financial records, then lucidly and simply explain them to a jury. A poised and beautiful young woman, Poon as a financial investigator and analyst approached genius. Hodges, a tall redhead with very blue eyes, was a twenty-five-year-old trainee. But she so industriously and effectively committed herself that she was inducted full time into the investigation.

The IRS team set out to build a classic tax case by tracing cash outlays and through them proving that Whitworth and his wife spent far more than they legitimately earned. By disclosing when Whitworth received cash from Walker, the pay record pointed investigators to periods in which they were most likely to find the outlays. Records seized and items observed in Whitworth's home provided other leads.

For example, found in Whitworth's home was a copy of a cable his wife sent him April 25, 1983, on the *Enterprise* as the carrier headed for home port. It said:

My darling, I passed. At present I feel exhausted, and triumph is not sweet without you. I long to have you home. Look for

the white 1957 Rolls Royce, a chauffeur and me, the lady in
red. Come Thursday a.m. I'm going to show you how a real
homecoming should be. The back seat of a Rolls is only the
beginning. So get some rest. You've got a meeting with destiny.
Smack, smack. Your Yearning Woman.

Like a leopard, Seddio pounced on the words "Rolls
Royce" and "a chauffeur." He found, sure enough, that Whitworth's wife in April 1983 hired a chauffeur and Rolls-Royce
to take him home from the ship. Then he discovered a $438.78
cash payment for rental of a Rolls-Royce in September 1983,
when the *Enterprise* again came home. He also recorded a
cash tip of $20.00 to the chauffeur.

A cable from Whitworth to his wife in March 1983 advised,
"Buy Krugerrands. Use discretion." This led Seddio to a
$4,380.00 cash purchase of Krugerrands.

Receipts found in Whitworth's home prompted an IRS inquiry to Victoria's Secret, a store specializing in the sale of
seductive lingerie. Indeed, it had a record of $1,600.00 in pur-
chases by Jerry Whitworth for female lingerie, including one
cash payment of $841.37.

Whitworth had a cockatoo, a rare kind of parrot. Suspecting
that such a bird was expensive, Seddio asked a veterinarian
how much one would cost. The veterinarian declined to say
on grounds that disclosure of the price might violate the "doc-
tor-patient relationship" between him and cockatoos. Nevertheless, Seddio persevered and ascertained that the Whit-
worths' cockatoo cost $900.00.

The cash outlays, large and small, added up: $21.50 auto
repairs; $2,500.00 Honda motorcycle; $724.19 dishwasher;
$5,000.00 deposit Wells Fargo Bank; $1,600.00 Bowles Hopkins Art Gallery; $16,650.00 bank deposits during four days
in February 1983.

According to the pay and other records, Walker on June 1,

1980, delivered $100,000.00 to Whitworth. Seddio, Poon, Hodges, "the Fong," and Hobbs documented cash outlays by Whitworth during the next seven months totaling $83,268.17.

As a result of the skill and ingenuity of the IRS investigators, Farmer and Schoggen by July were confident of successfully prosecuting Whitworth on charges of income tax evasion. However, they worried about the espionage charges and the remainder of the case. So did Martin and Dion. In late July, Martin flew to San Francisco to confer.

Nobody could ask more than the FBI had done thus far. In little more than three weeks, without any cooperation from the major principals, it had charted fairly precisely the workings of an espionage ring for the preceding ten years. It had not proved what had been stolen, but it had shown much of what could have been stolen. A good assumption was that spies as hard-working as Walker and Whitworth would steal all they could.

The espionage case against Whitworth, though, remained entirely circumstantial. The interrelationship and implications of the complex circumstances would be difficult for lay jurors to understand. And even the circumstantial case rested on evidence of dubious admissibility. The key evidence, the pay record, for example, consisted of two sheets of paper bearing cryptic letters and numerals without any visible link to Jerry Whitworth.

"Of course, if John Walker would testify," Farmer observed, "all our problems would be solved. Everything would be admissible."

"No chance of a deal," Martin said. "Lehman [Secretary of the Navy John F. Lehman, Jr.] wants blood, wants to hang him or put him away for a thousand years without any hint of a concession."

"I would like to do the same to Jerry Whitworth," Farmer said. "But if we want to deter spies, we at least must convict him of espionage. It will be a national debacle if we fail. Right now, I can't promise success."

There was another apparent drift in the case even more alarming than the prosecution's difficulties. The *Washington Post* quoted a ranking Pentagon official as saying that the losses inflicted by the Walker spy ring were "serious" but "not disastrous." The newspaper story added, "Other high-ranking Pentagon officials said yesterday they shared that assessment." A sentence buried near the end of the story said, "Whitworth's access to the most sensitive material would have been limited."

Senator David F. Durenberger, chairman of the Senate Intelligence Committee, suggested that the information to which the spy ring had access was not all that important. "I'm not that worried about the information. It certainly wasn't helpful [for it] to end up in Soviet hands, but it wasn't of such significance that there's any kind of alarm."

It was as if Washington officialdom had been transported to a serene land of fantasy impervious to sinister facts.

During the San Francisco conference between Martin and the prosecution team, Lieutenant Alsup kept quiet as befits a junior subordinate in the presence of distinguished superiors. As they left a meeting, Martin said to him, "Jim, I hear nothing but praise for you. I can't tell you how glad we are to have you with us. What do you think about the case?"

"Sir, I think something bad is happening. I think in Washington they're covering up or not facing the facts. I'm not an expert. But I know something about crypto and communications. I'll tell you, if we knew one tenth as much about Soviet crypto and communications as Whitworth could have told them about ours, then the Soviets wouldn't have any secrets from us. I think there's been a catastrophe, and we're not doing nearly enough about it."

Martin appreciated that the serious young lieutenant had

nothing to gain and perhaps much to lose by speaking as he did, and he was impressed. "I'm not sure I understand. Could you explain?"

"Do you have an hour?"

"I have all night if necessary."

They adjourned to Leida Schoggen's office, and Alsup reviewed for Martin each of Whitworth's duty assignments, explaining the data he could have stolen at each and how the Soviets could have exploited the secrets.

At the conclusion, Martin summed up his understanding. "You mean the Soviets may have built duplicates of our machines and with the keys read all the traffic, that they might have learned enough to read the traffic without the keys?"

"Yes, sir."

"Then they could still be reading it?"

"That's possible, sir."

"Holy shit!"

8

Revelations
from Moscow

SHORTLY AFTER John Martin returned from San Francisco in late July, the CIA informed him that someone
he never expected to hear of again was in Washington.
His name was Vitaly Sergeyevich Yurchenko. And Yurchenko
possessed something Martin never expected to receive: the
KGB perspective on the Walker case.

Martin had met the Russian several times while Yurchenko
was security officer at the Soviet embassy in Washington from
1975 to May 1980. Their encounters usually occurred at Danker's, on E Street near the National Theater. Although it is a
downtown bar and grill, Danker's has the congenial, sometimes roisterous atmosphere of a neighborhood pub. Many of
its patrons are judges, Justice Department lawyers, and FBI,
IRS, Secret Service, and Customs agents who convene after
work to trade jokes and professional gossip.

Yurchenko loved to drink Scotch with them and be accepted into their company. For a man who began life on a
mean collective farm, his father killed in the siege of Leningrad, his mother toiling in the fields, Yurchenko looked on
Danker's as an oasis in a long and often brutal journey. It of-

fered a relaxed camaraderie that his work for many years had denied him.

No matter what his personal qualities, the security officer in any Soviet colony abroad is feared by most and despised by many of his wards. All know that he directs the pervasive network of informants who spy and pry into everybody's private life, that his disfavor can bring a one-way ticket to home and ruin. Operational KGB officers, who consider that they are doing "a real man's job," are contemptuous of someone who devotes his working day to petty stool pigeons, malicious rumors, and finding out who is sleeping with whom. While the security officer can command outward deference, he cannot count on having many friends.

Yurchenko was no exception. Alex Costa in the late 1970s was the wife of a first secretary at the embassy. When her husband returned to Moscow, she chose to remain with their two children in the United States. She recalls the raw fear the mere sight of Yurchenko aroused. "Be careful of him," her husband warned. "He is very dangerous."

Yurchenko, however, had additional, more respectable duties that included liaison with the FBI. Their natural, irreconcilable enmity notwithstanding, the FBI and KGB sometimes exchange information regarding certain limited matters of mutual interest to their respective governments. Yurchenko passed whatever the Soviets elected to give and accepted whatever the FBI provided. He also consulted the FBI regarding physical protection of the embassy, its staff, and visiting Soviet dignitaries. Thus, in their hours together he and FBI agents suspended combat. And paradoxically, during these hours with enemies who did not fear him, he could afford to be more himself than he could at the embassy.

Normally, Yurchenko came to Danker's with one of the FBI agents designated to deal with him. On a wintry evening as he and an agent stood at the far end of the bar, Martin stepped in out of the snow. The agent called, "John, come meet a friend." Introducing Martin, he said, "John's the man who puts your spies in jail."

In a tone of mock confidence, Yurchenko responded, "Always he is trying to fan the flames of Cold War and spy mania. He knows we have no spies." All three laughed, Yurchenko the loudest.

As they chatted, Yurchenko affably asked, "How do you like my suit? I just bought it. You think I look American?" It was a dark three-piece suit, expensive and well tailored. In it, Yurchenko, who had the strong, good-looking face of a peasant, with dark eyes and a bushy mustache that drooped around the corners of his mouth, looked quite distinguished.

"It's an elegant suit," Martin replied. "I wish I had one like it. But, Vitaly, if you want to look like an American, you're going to have to get rid of that silly furry hat there."

Yurchenko insisted on paying the check. Clearly, he wanted to be liked, and Martin found it hard not to like him.

They chanced to meet again in late February or early March 1980, and Yurchenko announced he would depart for Moscow soon. Martin said, "Vitaly, I wish all good for you in your personal life. I hope you have a terrible time professionally."

Yurchenko smiled and said, "Thank you, John."

Back in Moscow, Yurchenko became chief of the Fifth Department of Directorate K, which was charged with a host of counterintelligence responsibilities: investigating foreign espionage inside the KGB; analyzing why given KGB operations had been disrupted, agents arrested, and officers exposed; investigating defections by KGB officers and tracking down defectors abroad; ascertaining the sources of leaks of information from within the KGB; working with foreign intelligence personnel who defected to the Soviet Union; and using special drugs and chemicals for surveillance, incapacitation, or assassination.

The KGB in April 1985 made Yurchenko deputy chief of the First Department of the First Chief Directorate. This department supervises KGB residencies, or outposts, in Washington, New York, San Francisco, and Ottawa; assists all other KGB elements in operations against Americans throughout the world; and coordinates operations of the East European and Cuban intelligence services against the United States.

Neither of these two appointments placed Yurchenko in the highest leadership of the KGB. There were many dozens, maybe as many as two hundred men above him. The positions, though, were important, and most officers would have been happy to occupy either.

On June 28, 1985, Yurchenko landed in Rome, ostensibly to persuade Italian authorities to allow him to talk to a Soviet scientist who had defected after attending a nuclear disarmament conference. On August 1 he strode out of the Soviet embassy, telling colleagues he intended to visit the Vatican museum. Instead, he presented himself at the U.S. embassy and asked for asylum in the United States. He explained that he loathed his duties in the KGB, longed for life in America, was trapped in a miserable marriage, and dreamed of reunion with the woman he truly loved, a Soviet diplomat's wife with whom he had an affair in Washington and who now was in Canada.

As might be expected, Yurchenko brought with him an enormous volume of intelligence. The most urgent concerned the KGB resident in London, Oleg Gorzdievski. According to Yurchenko, the KGB strongly suspected Gorzdievski of treason, of being an active agent of some Western intelligence service. He, along with his family, had been recalled to Moscow for "consultations." At the moment, he was the object of subtle yet intensive investigation. The KGB had to be circumspect because the party had put an end to the days when senior members could be shot on whim. To falsely accuse someone of such lofty standing as a resident would be disastrous for the accusers. But in Yurchenko's opinion, the KGB before long would ascertain that Gorzdievski in fact was guilty, arrest him, wrench out a confession, and execute him.

Gorzdievski was not an American agent. The CIA figured that if he belonged to anybody, it would be the British. So it told them. They in effect said: Interesting. Thank you very much. Then, overnight, they went to work.

Incredibly, the British snatched Gorzdievski out of the very maw of the KGB. They smuggled him from Moscow and across the Soviet Union and Europe to London. There, the British announced his defection and the expulsion of thirty-one KGB officers, virtually the entire London residency.

Those who suspected Gorzdievski were right. According to the later public statement of a Danish intelligence official, he first entered into an alliance with the British in 1972 in Copenhagen, although the date may or may not be accurate; it is certain that when Gorzdievski arrived in London in 1983 to be deputy resident, then resident, he already was a loyal agent of Her Majesty's Secret Service, MI-6.

After Gorzdievski's sensational escape, the KGB had to wonder. Through all the years, what had he revealed to the perfidious English? Were any of the hundreds of officers with whom he associated along the way contaminated? What should be done to clear up the wreckage he had undoubtedly wrought? Precise answers would be hard to come by because Gorzdievski was gone.

However, as Yurchenko pointed out, to the parasitical careerists, the members of the Nomenklatura in the KGB, his absence would be a relief. It would spare them the full consequences of the truths a confession would have bared. The damage could be minimized, explained away, covered up, and far fewer people would suffer. The Soviet Union, of course, would suffer. But a real Nomenklaturist cares about Soviet interests only to the extent that they coincide with the preservation and aggrandizement of his own.

Yurchenko also illuminated a dark case the CIA had hoped to settle by itself, without the embarrassment of exposing family skeletons to outsiders such as the FBI and Justice Department. But by September, analysis of Yurchenko's reports convinced the CIA it had no choice except to tell the full story to both. It was not a pretty story.

In January 1981 the CIA hired as a probationary staff officer Edward Lee Howard, thirty-two, who recently had received a master's degree in business administration from American University in Washington. The son of a career air force sergeant, Howard was born in New Mexico; took an undergraduate degree from the University of Texas; spent four years in the Peace Corps, part of the time in Latin America, then three years in Peru with the Agency for International Development before beginning graduate studies.

Like those of the FBI and National Security Agency, CIA employment standards are exceedingly stringent; only a small minority of applicants are accepted. The standards, however, are applied by fallible humans. Howard demonstrated high intelligence, and he had proved his ability to master languages and work effectively in foreign environments. So the CIA employed him, although in the preemployment examinations, which included a polygraph test, Howard admitted to using drugs.

Soon the CIA began to train Howard to service American agents in Moscow, the most difficult and dangerous operational theater in the world. He learned to use sophisticated disguises and ingenious techniques by which the CIA was able to communicate securely with agents despite constant KGB surveillance. The training included practical indoctrination by a crack FBI team in methods of recognizing and eluding surveillance.

Each officer of the CIA clandestine service must submit to another polygraph examination before departing for a foreign post. The examination of Howard indicated that he was being deceptive about a number of issues. It turned out that he suffered from acute alcohol and drug problems as well as emotional instability. The CIA fired him in summer 1983, and he moved to Santa Fe, New Mexico, and found a job with the state legislature. In 1984 he pleaded guilty to assault with a deadly weapon after firing a .44 magnum pistol during a melee with three men. He received a five-year suspended sentence.

To its credit, the CIA later offered Howard, at government expense, counseling by a psychiatrist and one of its experienced operational officers. During the counseling, Howard disclosed that he had entertained the idea of avenging his dismissal by selling all he knew to the KGB. He even had gone so far as to loiter in Lafayette Park debating whether to walk into the Soviet embassy not far away. However, he claimed that he stopped short of actually contacting the KGB.

Beginning in 1984, CIA operations in Moscow started to sour. Now, in 1985, Yurchenko explained that their demise resulted from leads provided by a former CIA employee whose true name he did not know. He did recall that the KGB considered the American an alcoholic or drug addict.

Because of possible effects on its own operations, the FBI alerted some of its offices, including San Francisco, to grim questions about Howard. Bill Smits at once concluded that the case should not be handled by ordinary methods because Howard was no ordinary spy. He was, rather, the recipient of the best espionage training the United States could provide. Smits had in mind a ploy involving Russian-speaking FBI agents, which had succeeded in San Francisco several times.

Aware that the FBI's Santa Fe office had little experience in counterintelligence against the KGB, Smits called and offered to lend some of his best men. The Santa Fe agent who took the call expressed appreciation and said he would be back in touch. But a Santa Fe supervisor soon sent angry word through headquarters that Smits should stay the hell away and mind his own goddamned business.

At Martin's behest, Justice Department attorneys prepared a secret complaint charging Howard with espionage. Meanwhile, the Santa Fe office tapped his telephone and placed him and his home under twenty-four-hour surveillance.

But as U.S. intelligence later learned, the KGB already had forewarned Howard. On August 3, two days after Yurchenko defected, Howard clandestinely conferred with the Soviets in Vienna. They advised him that they had just lost an officer who probably knew about his collaboration with them. Handing him $100,000, they assured him that he and his family were welcome in the Soviet Union. If he elected to remain in the United States, the KGB would do what it could to help him. But he would be very much at risk in America. So Howard now was on guard.

On the night of September 20, 1985, Howard made two telephone calls, one to a baby sitter and another to a restaurant requesting reservations. The calls should have warned monitors that he was about to leave the house. They did not. Surveillants watching through closed-circuit television should have seen him leave. They did not. Other surveillants parked outside the lone entrance to his housing subdivision should have seen him drive away. They missed him. Howard vanished to Moscow, the first CIA defector ever to flee to the Soviet Union.*

Yurchenko additionally advised that the KGB had been obtaining extraordinarily valuable intelligence from a former employee of the National Security Agency. But Yurchenko's

---

*There is one consolation, small though it may be. Howard is a highly disturbed, raving addict prone to violence. For the KGB, handling him will be an edifying experience.

knowledge was sparse. He remembered that he himself had participated in a telephone conversation with the American sometime early in 1980 when he called to make arrangements to visit the Soviet embassy. And Yurchenko believed that the caller later did come to the embassy. That was all he could say.

According to a widely accepted myth, the FBI detects anyone who telephones the Soviet embassy and, by photograph, identifies anybody who visits it. Unless someone in a phone conversation lets slip identifying clues or unless monitors hear a voice with which they happen to be familiar, the FBI cannot identify a person solely on the basis of a telephone call. Each workday, hundreds of people go in and out of the Soviet embassy, almost all in consequence of perfectly legal business. The FBI cannot possibly trail all of them to ascertain who they are. The prevailing myth assumes that the FBI can photograph each and every person entering or leaving the embassy around the clock; for various reasons, it cannot. Even if it could, a photograph by itself would not suffice to identify an individual unless agents studying it already knew him or her by sight. The picture would have to be matched with other data, which might or might not be available or retrievable.

The FBI, however, did retain tapes of telephone calls made to the embassy as far back as 1980. Sorting out those on which Yurchenko's voice was recorded, it located a tape of the conversation he had had with the unknown American caller on January 14, 1980. Eventually, NSA supervisors recognized the American voice as that of Ronald William Pelton, who resigned from the agency in 1979 after fourteen years of employment.

As Pelton subsequently confessed, he went to the embassy on January 15, 1980, and agreed to sell NSA secrets and to meet the KGB later in Vienna. The Soviets instructed him to shave off his beard and put on clothes similar to those worn by embassy workers. They then put him in a bus that shuttles workers between the embassy and their residential compound. There, over dinner, they further debriefed him before spiriting him back downtown. Later, during prolonged interrogations in Vienna, he revealed to the KGB all he knew about NSA operations and successes against the Soviet Union. The NSA adjudged the damage horrendous.*

With the escape of Howard and the confession of Pelton, it remained for the CIA and NSA to clean up the messes or, as John le Carré might say, "put the paste back in the tube." But there were other Yurchenko revelations that still chilled and preoccupied Martin: They pertained to John Walker and Jerry Whitworth.

According to Yurchenko, the KGB did not believe that Walker's arrest resulted from disclosures by his former wife. To cynical Soviet analysts it made no sense. If Barbara Walker really knew about her former husband's espionage and was disposed to destroy him, why would she wait seventeen years? And whatever her feelings toward Walker, would she actually doom her own son to prison? No. The story that Barbara informed on Walker was a legend, an FBI ruse to protect the Soviet traitor who betrayed the ring.

The Soviet disbelief was ironic. At FBI request, Martin and Dion had tried to mask the roles of Barbara and Laura Walker. In the first draft of the presentation composed for submission to a grand jury, they referred to them only as cooperating sources who were well informed. The FBI desired to spare them the disruption of their personal lives that publicity would cause for as long as possible. More important, the FBI wanted to confuse the KGB and force Walker to speculate about

*A federal jury in Baltimore, Maryland, on June 5, 1986, convicted Pelton of espionage. Despite his cooperation with government investigators after conviction, Pelton was sentenced to life in prison in December 1986.

whether a confederate or defector had betrayed him. Unfortunately, an FBI spokesman shortly after Walker's arrest blurted out the facts about Barbara and Laura.

During his years at the Washington residency and KGB headquarters, Yurchenko had gleaned not a hint of the Walker espionage ring. Department 16 of the First Chief Directorate conducted the operation in such compartmentalized secrecy that only a few people were aware of it. Even the specially selected officers sent to Washington solely to service Walker's drops did not know with whom they were dealing or what he was providing.

Because the KGB did not believe the FBI story about Barbara and Laura, it called upon Yurchenko to review the case and determine who sold out. On the basis of verbal briefings and portions of the case file that he read before his trip to Rome, Yurchenko reported:

• The KGB regarded the Walker-Whitworth case as the greatest in its history, surpassing in import even the Soviet theft of Anglo-American blueprints for the first atomic bomb.

• The cryptographic data supplied by Walker and Whitworth enabled the Soviets to decipher "more than a million" or "millions" of secret American messages.

• The three principal officers who supervised the case received the highest Soviet decorations.

• One of the senior KGB officers who briefed Yurchenko stated that in event of war, this Soviet ability to read enciphered American messages would be "devastating" to the United States.

Nothing previously disclosed in the investigation affected Martin as much as Yurchenko's revelations. He trusted Smits's judgments, and Lieutenant Alsup impressed him. But it was one thing for Smits and Peterson to *believe,* as they did as early as 1984, that the country was in dire peril, or for Alsup to *theorize,* as he did in talking to Martin in San Francisco, that a catastrophe had occurred. It was quite another to hear virtually the same assessment from the Soviets themselves.

Martin thought about his duty. He stood now at the apex of government civil service, his record festooned with awards, commendations, bonuses. He had heard that he might receive the 1985 award as the most outstanding among the Justice Department's sixty-eight thousand employees. In speculation about who might be selected as the next FBI director when William H. Webster's ten-year term expired in 1988, his name was sometimes mentioned.

As chief of the Internal Security Section, he was responsible for overseeing the successful prosecution of Jerry Whitworth, and he had no obligation to provoke controversy and incur enmity by exceeding that responsibility. He could not be faulted if the Defense Department and intelligence community refused to face up to the damage Walker and Whitworth had wrought and thereby failed to set things right. That was their responsibility, not his. If a jury acquitted Whitworth, well, he, Dion, Farmer, and Leida would have done their best with what they had. The government had won every espionage case in which he had been involved in the past ten years. You're bound to lose one now and then.

All this was sophistry, Martin realized. If he had cause to believe that the government was making a calamitous mistake that he might rectify, then duty bound him to do all he honorably could to rectify it. And Martin knew there was something he might do.

If John Walker could be induced to talk and to testify against Whitworth, to specify all that he and, more significantly, Whitworth gave the Soviets, then nobody could hide from the facts. Everybody would see exactly what had been lost and, presumably, what had to be done to make amends. Cost, sloth, inertia, pride, dogmatic theory, could not stand in the way of repairs.

Privately, Martin canvassed acquaintances in the navy and NSA. Was a detailed accounting from the Walkers really necessary? Should a deal with John Walker be attempted? The answers were unanimous: Hell, yes! Do it if you can.

There was no question of granting any substantive concessions to John Walker himself. He had to be sentenced to life imprisonment, and he understood that. But from a prison cell Michael Walker had been writing pitiful pleas: Dad, you got me into this. For God's sake, do something to get me out. Martin thought that John Walker might be motivated to cooperate if his son were guaranteed a negotiated sentence of less than life. And he reasoned that a sentence for Michael of, say, twenty-five years would be both practicable and justifiable.

Even if the government prosecuted Michael to the fullest, there was no certainty that a judge would put him away for life or, for that matter, as long as twenty-five years. A skillful defense attorney would argue, with some validity, that Michael was the hapless pawn, the mesmerized victim of a diabolical and overpowering father. In setting sentence, a judge very well might be swayed by this argument. There was another consideration. Because of heretofore lenient parole policies, few criminals serve their full sentence. Convicted spies, though, are different. Parole boards rarely defy Justice Department recommendations, which always oppose the parole of a spy. So if Michael Walker agreed to a twenty-five-year sentence, he probably would serve the full twenty-five years, just as John Walker probably would remain incarcerated for life.

On his own initiative, Martin asked Michael Schatzow, the

assistant U.S. attorney in Baltimore assigned to prosecute John and Michael Walker, to sound out their attorneys. Schatzow did not want to negotiate; he wanted to go to trial. But once he understood the rationale of Martin's request, he loyally acquiesced. Soon he reported that Walker was ready to tell all and to testify against Whitworth if the government would spare Michael a life sentence.

But a formidable obstacle to an agreement remained in the person of John F. Lehman, Jr., the most popular and, many would argue, the best secretary of the navy since World War II. Intelligent, handsome, outspoken, youthful, and independently wealthy, Lehman comported himself with the dash and flair of the navy aviator he is. He had confronted head-on previously unassailable defense contractors he felt were bilking the navy and taxpayers. Under his stewardship, the navy had curtailed drug abuse to relatively minuscule levels, and morale had soared. He had adeptly presided over a dramatic build-up and modernization of the fleet whose advanced new weapons worked to perfection in repelling Libyan assaults in the Gulf of Sidra. And, as Washington cognoscenti knew, he enjoyed the personal esteem and confidence of President Reagan.

After the arrests of the three Walkers and Whitworth, Lehman was enraged. He made noises about recalling the three retirees to active naval duty so they could be prosecuted in courts-martial. He implied that the Justice Department and civilian courts indolently dealt with espionage as they would any ordinary white-collar crime.

In fact, never in modern peacetime history had the Justice Department prosecuted espionage cases as vigorously as it had since 1975, and the record clearly demonstrates that, for comparable offenses, military courts almost invariably impose lighter sentences than civilian courts.

Be that as it may, Lehman adamantly and aggressively opposed any agreement with the Walkers and any sentence for Michael of less than life.

Fortunately for him, Martin had a perceptive and courageous boss, Stephen Trott, assistant attorney general for the Criminal Division. A former prosecutor and U.S. attorney in Los Angeles, Trott shared Lehman's loathing for the Walkers. He understood what Lehman felt for the half-million men and women of the navy whose lives they had jeopardized. But his own appraisal of the pending cases and the damage convinced him that the interests of the armed forces and the nation best would be served by securing the collaboration of the traitors. On October 21, he and Martin went together to the Pentagon and a showdown.

In the office of Secretary of Defense Caspar Weinberger, Martin and Lehman laid down the opposing arguments. When Martin stated that John Walker's cooperation was essential to ensure conviction of Whitworth, Lehman interrupted and angrily declared, "I don't care if Whitworth walks." That was a mistake.

Weinberger raised his eyebrows in surprise, then his hand in a signal for silence. "Wait a minute," he said. "You mean you might not be able to convict Whitworth?"

Martin explained the weaknesses in the government's case arising from the probable inadmissibility of critical evidence. He further explained that testimony by Walker would make the documentary evidence admissible and almost guarantee a conviction. Weinberger, himself a lawyer, grasped everything. Addressing the assembled group as a whole but looking at Lehman, he said, "I'll get back to you tomorrow."

The next day the Pentagon sent Martin a message of one word: "Consummate."

On October 28, 1985, in Baltimore federal court, John and

152

Michael Walker pleaded guilty to espionage. Their attorneys announced they had agreed to sentences of life and twenty-five years. In return, both pledged to cooperate fully and truthfully with the government and to testify against Whitworth. The judge delayed formal sentencing indefinitely pending their fulfillment of the agreement.

A reporter asked if John Walker might not be paroled after serving ten or twelve years. "It's theoretically possible, just as it's possible this building might fall on us," Schatzow replied. "I think the chances of both happening are about the same."

In statements to the press, Secretary Lehman denounced the agreement. "We in the navy are disappointed at the plea bargain," he said. "It continues a tradition in the Justice Department of treating espionage as just another white-collar crime, and we think that it should be in a very different category." He added that "the acts were traitorous acts and ought to be treated differently than insider trading." Lehman also asserted that Walker's information was not essential to a damage assessment.

Two days later, on November 1, Weinberger issued an unprecedented rebuke. "Secretary Lehman now understands that he did not have all the facts concerning the matter before he made several injudicious and incorrect statements with respect to the agreement," it said.

"Secretary Lehman now has all the facts and is in complete agreement with the government's decision."

The Weinberger statement further emphasized that Lehman now understood that the sentences agreed upon were "fully as severe as could have been obtained" through prosecution. Martin was elated.

Farmer and Schoggen together with FBI agents and navy investigators already had begun the interrogation of Walker in a Baltimore jail. At the outset, Walker said to them, "You wanna know what happened? Just figure it this way. If I had access to it, color it gone."

On Saturday night, November 2, Vitaly Yurchenko and a lone CIA escort in his early twenties dined at Au Pied de Cochon, a noisy, mediocre restaurant in northwest Washington. Everything about the evening was wrong.

The young escort spoke no Russian and knew nothing about the Soviet Union or the KGB and almost nothing about his guest. He was half Yurchenko's age, and in Russian culture it is difficult for an elder to relate to someone many years his junior. By assigning such an escort and only one escort, the CIA implied to Yurchenko that he now was a nobody who did not merit the company of important people. On a Saturday night, important CIA people had better things to do than waste time with a lousy Russian defector who, having been squeezed dry like a lemon, now could be discarded with the garbage.

Yurchenko had asked to dine at a French restaurant, doubtless envisioning elegant ambience, splendid wines, and delectable cuisine. Washington abounds with such restaurants; the escort was not familiar with any of them. So from the telephone directory he at random picked Au Pied de Cochon, a further insult. And Au Pied de Cochon is an easy fifteen-minute walk from the Soviet residential compound at Mount Alto.

"If I walked out of here, would you shoot me?" Yurchenko asked.

"No."

"Well, if I'm not back in fifteen minutes, it's not your fault."

It did not occur to the CIA escort to ask where Yurchenko intended to go. Nor did it occur to him to ask whether Yurchenko was experiencing difficulties with which he or others might help. He dumbly sat there while Yurchenko walked away, never to return.

On Monday, November 4, the Soviet embassy welcomed American journalists to a rare press conference, starring a tense and nervous Vitaly Yurchenko. He announced that he had escaped the clutches of the CIA after having been drugged and abducted in Rome, then dragooned to the United States and held captive for three months by deranged "torturers." Prompted by a Soviet journalist, he agreed that, yes, he was a victim of "state terrorism." Now that the terrible ordeal had ended, he wanted to return home to his loving family and get back to work. The Soviets delivered a pious protest to the State Department, decrying the barbarities visited on one of their innocent citizens.

Back in Moscow, Yurchenko, still nervous and accompanied by a physician, appeared in a propaganda circus. "Every day they gave me tablets and narcotics. My tormenters looked on me as an animal in a zoo," he declared. "They told me that if I did not cooperate, I would end my life a madman." As everyone could see, Yurchenko emerged from this excruciating torment looking remarkably fit. But he explained. "They made me play golf. They also let me get a suntan to change the greenish color of my face."

The theatrical flight of Yurchenko persuaded some members of Congress that he was a phony defector planted by the KGB for nefarious purposes. They believed that no genuine defector of Yurchenko's stature voluntarily would put himself at the mercy of the KGB. Neither, they said, would the Soviets allow anyone in whom they reposed less than complete confidence to speak at a public press conference.

Proponents of the false-defector theory argued that Howard and Pelton, indisputably exposed by Yurchenko, represented burned-out cases. Neither was in government any longer nor in a position to provide useful intelligence. The KGB already had taken all they had to give. Therefore, it could afford to let Yurchenko sacrifice them in order to build credibility. As these proponents were ignorant of Yurchenko's role in saving Gorzdievski's life, they did not discuss it.

What did the Soviets expect to gain by sending Yurchenko on his American odyssey? According to the skeptics, his redefection was preplanned to embarrass and weaken the Reagan administration on the eve of the first summit conference with Mikhail Gorbachev. His redefection was calculated to deter prospective KGB defectors by dramatizing the impossibility of life in the United States for a Russian. By stating that he knew of no existing penetrations of American intelligence, he could lull the CIA, FBI, and others into complacency and perhaps thereby protect high-level agents who might still be at work. By artfully analyzing the questions put to him by his American interrogators, he could discern what the CIA did and did not know and thereby acquire clues as to its penetrations in Moscow.

Senior CIA and FBI officials who are aware of the totality of what Yurchenko provided remain convinced that he was authentic. They point out that polygraph examinations indicated he was truthful and that everything verifiable in his information has proved valid. He fled, they believe, because of any one of a number of factors or combination thereof: incompetence by those responsible for his resettlement; anguish at being spurned by the paramour with whom he dreamed of creating a new life; deep depression that often afflicts Russian expatriates; irrational impulse.

"We have opened a substantial number of cases based on very useful information he has supplied," FBI Director William H. Webster stated publicly. "Not only new cases, but reviewing old information that might reflect on other holes that were open in prior years." Webster added that for the Soviets it would have been "an act of folly" to give up all

Yurchenko supplied merely in the hope of embarrassing the United States.

In all the propaganda bombasts, Yurchenko uttered not one disparaging word about the FBI. If he is still alive, his acquaintances from Danker's wish him well, for, whatever his motivations, he performed a great service to the United States. His revelations about the Walker case provided the stimulus for the actions that ultimately enabled American investigators to look inside the spy ring and see its inner workings over a span of seventeen years. And what they saw would adrenalize U.S. efforts to take away the "devastating" advantage the ring had given to the Soviet Union.

9

Inside the Ring

BOB HUNTER, JIM KOLOUCH, John Peterson, Bob Griego, Buck Farmer, Leida Schoggen, and numerous naval officers interrogated John Walker over many months at many places, mainly at FBI offices in Baltimore and San Francisco and the federal prison in downtown San Diego.

Often, even though cooperating with the government, a criminal instinctively tries to minimize his crimes and thereby his guilt. Not John Walker.

From the first day, he nonchalantly and sometimes proudly recounted his feats of espionage. And he peppered his narrative with irreverent or cynical asides.

Emphasizing that his private detective business was legitimate, he remarked, "I was making fifty thousand honest dollars a year when you arrested me — you pricks."

Concerning his accurate prediction to the KGB that Whitworth eventually would decide to rejoin the ring, he said, "Deep in my black heart, I knew that miserable shit couldn't hack it on the outside."

Discussing his efforts to recruit his daughter Laura as a spy, he explained, "She was starving. I wanted to get her some money and bring her back into the mainstream of American life." And he liked American life. "I'm very patriotic. I've only committed one crime in my life."

Regarding the unpredictability of juries, he opined, "Yeah, those fucking fruitcake jurors in California are likely to let him [Whitworth] go."

Walker wanted Jerry Whitworth to be convicted. Upon reading the RUS letters, he instantly recognized Whitworth as the author. And he never forgave Whitworth for even considering the idea of betraying him and the rest.

Nevertheless, Farmer and Schoggen always worried about whether Walker was telling the truth. Whitworth's lawyers would labor mightily to portray him as a totally dishonorable and therefore unbelievable witness. If the defense could catch Walker in a significant lie, it might succeed in undermining the entire government case in the minds of the jurors.

So concurrently with the interrogation, the FBI undertook an intensive investigation in an effort to corroborate what Walker said. From the records of travel agencies, airlines, hotels, and credit card companies, it traced his journeys through the years to prove that he was where he said when he said. By reviewing his visits to safety deposit boxes, it compiled circumstantial evidence in support of his reports of payments to Whitworth. No detail was too small to merit examination. For example, Walker stated that the KGB eventually stopped supplying Minox camera film and that Whitworth had to buy his own. Acting on a lead from Peterson, the New York field office ascertained that in 1982 Whitworth ordered a huge quantity of Minox film from a New York shop.

Some of Walker's statements, such as those describing his personal meetings and conversations with KGB officers, could not be checked. But Farmer brought in independent experts, including former KGB major Stanislav Levchenko, and asked them: Is this plausible? Is this the way the KGB would do it? Why?

Reports of the ongoing interrogations and investigation, together with a succession of advisers from the FBI, NSA, and navy in Washington, all came to Farmer's office on the sixteenth floor of the Federal Building. Though sterile in its government furnishings, the office commanded a majestic view of San Francisco. And Farmer kept his thirty-thousand-dollar secure red phone on the window ledge so he could enjoy the unsurpassed vistas while talking to John Martin or John Dion in Washington, as he did almost daily.

He and Leida worked seven days a week through summer 1985 and into spring 1986, taking off Sundays only at Thanksgiving, Christmas, and Easter. Generally, they stopped work each day at about 6:00 P.M. to swim and exercise at the Olympic Club and the YMCA. Afterward, Farmer would drive over Nob Hill to Chinatown and buy a fresh salmon or tuna. Whoever was in town would bring the chardonnay, and while dinner was being prepared they all would stand in the kitchen of Farmer's apartment, perched on a slope near Golden Gate Park, reviewing the case. Since almost every night in San Francisco is cool irrespective of the season, the collective analysis usually continued after dinner around a wood fire.

By March 1986 they had reconstructed in vast detail the history of the ring. Even John Walker, who was openly disdainful of the FBI for not having caught him earlier, paid a grudging compliment. "I'm amazed at how much you've found out." With a grin, he added, "Too bad for you that you didn't find out a lot earlier." Farmer and Schoggen were sure of most of what Walker had told them. They were totally sure of all he said about Jerry Whitworth.

John Walker professed not to know exactly why he did it.

In Richmond, Virginia, and Scranton, Pennsylvania, he had a miserable childhood, benighted by parental alcoholism and separation. And he was drifting into crime when brother Arthur rescued him and dragged him into the navy. Trained as a radioman, he considered his first duty aboard a submarine tender "shitty." Transferred to diesel submarines, he disliked wearing the same clothes for fifty consecutive days. But he found service aboard nuclear submarines comfortable and stimulating.

Drawing on his native intelligence, he did very well. By passing tests, he received through the navy the equivalent of both high school and college diplomas, and in only ten years he rose from seaman recruit to warrant officer.

But in early 1968 Walker fell into acute depression. He was unhappy in his marriage. Failure of a little restaurant he had opened in South Carolina put him in debt. He felt that his duties as a communications watch officer on the Norfolk staff of the commander of submarine forces in the Atlantic (COMSUBLANT) were boring and useless. Life seemed arid and meaningless. He thought, "This whole world is a fucking joke."

One night on a dull watch, he listened to sailors joke about how they might sell secrets to the Soviets. "If I were going to do it, I'd sell crypto," one said. Walker likened the conversation to that of bank tellers idly bantering about embezzlement. But it affected him.

A couple of days later, on a dingy January afternoon, he drove toward Washington and the Soviet embassy. He thought it possible that the FBI would detect and arrest him outside the embassy. He believed that even if he went unnoticed and struck a deal with the Soviets, the FBI would arrest him within a year or so at the most. "Looking back, I think I had a death wish."

In Washington, Walker parked his car downtown, looked up the address of the embassy in a telephone booth directory, and took a taxi to the corner of Sixteenth and K streets, N.W. He walked past the embassy, a somber old mansion with heavily shuttered and armored windows topped by a forest of eavesdropping antennas, then went back and encountered a Russian, perhaps a chauffeur. "I want to talk to someone from security," he said.

Though surprised, the Russian escorted him inside and presented him to a receptionist and a man who led him down a corridor into a small office. Shortly, a KGB officer appeared. Whoever he was, he was an able and decisive officer.

A large percentage of people who walk into Soviet embassies unannounced and offer themselves as spies are mentally disturbed, swindlers, or provocateurs controlled by hostile counterintelligence services. To winnow out the few walk-ins with genuine potential as agents, the KGB has evolved fairly standard procedures. Unless the individual is obviously bonkers, the KGB officer listens noncommittally, takes whatever the person may have to offer, ascertains his or her professional circumstances and access, and tries to gather enough background data to facilitate a full investigation of the applicant. If the foreigner is of interest, the KGB officer will arrange means whereby the Soviets can contact him or her later should they so desire. During an initial meeting, the KGB almost never pays anyone a substantial amount of money, though it may disburse minor sums for expenses. The local KGB residency then does nothing pending receipt of an evaluation and instructions from the Center, or Moscow headquarters.

But once John Walker claimed to have continuous access to cryptographic secrets and proposed to sell them, the KGB in Washington abandoned the standard procedures.

To demonstrate his wares, Walker brought along a list containing thirty days of key settings for the KL-47 cipher machine, part of the Adonis system. The KL-47 was an older system relying upon rotors, and the navy used it for multiple purposes, including transmission of delicate personal messages. As Walker described it, "If they wanted to tell a ship's captain that his wife was screwing the delivery boy, they'd send on the KL-47." The security classifications Top Secret and SPECAT (Special Category) on the keylist, however, looked impressive, and that is why Walker selected it for exhibition purposes.

The KGB officer vanished with the keylist. Returning after about ten minutes, he asserted that the list was not authentic because it was unsigned. Walker explained that NSA some time ago stopped imprinting keylists with the signature of its director, and the Russian appeared to accept the explanation. He did not, though, accept the false name Walker had given. Demanding some identification, he said, "We will not deal with anyone whose identity we do not know." Walker handed over his naval identification card, and the Russian again went away for ten minutes or so. When he came back, the KGB had decided to deal.

The Russian wanted to know more exactly what Walker could provide, and he told him: complete data about the KWR-37 cipher system, the principal system employed to communicate with submarines and naval installations in Europe; comparable data about the KG-13, KL-11, and KL-47 cipher machines; copies of secret messages sent to submarines and surface ships supporting them in the Atlantic.

In return, Walker asked for one thousand dollars a week. Seemingly agreeing, the Russian gave him an advance of two thousand or three thousand (Walker cannot remember the specific amount) and precise instructions for a clandestine meeting a month later on a date Walker picked. The KGB officer insisted that Walker memorize the instructions. "I'm too nervous," Walker said as he wrote them down.

Around 6:00 P.M., approximately an hour after Walker en-

163

tered the embassy, the KGB bundled him in an overcoat and gave him a hat. Four men hurried him out the rear entrance and into a waiting car. With Russians on either side to conceal him in the back seat, the party commenced weaving through Washington checking for surveillance. Weary of the ceaseless meandering, Walker complained, "You assholes are going to make me late for my watch."

"It's for your own good," he was told. Finally, about 7:00 P.M., they let him out near his car.

The KGB on the spot had elected to gamble. It actually knew nothing about Walker. He, his identification card, and the keylist all could be fraudulent, though they looked genuine. He could be an agent of the FBI or one of the military intelligence services. If so, the KGB officer appointed to rendezvous with him in a month or so might be arrested, then or later. The resident and anyone else involved could expect, at a minimum, to be rebuked for poor judgment and disregard of standard procedures.

These risks were minuscule compared to the possible gains. That dark winter afternoon in January 1968, the KGB in Washington wholly comprehended what a retired NSA security director, Earl Clark, would later try to impart while instructing Farmer and Schoggen about cryptography. Clark put it this way: "Give me access to your codes, give me access to your ciphers, and you won't have any secrets. I don't have to steal the Stealth bomber plans. I don't have to know about your nuclear command controlling. I don't have to know about your diplomatic communications. If I can get access to your codes and ciphers, I have access to all your critical secrets. You cannot put a price on cryptography."

Walker either would produce the promised cryptographic data, or he would not. The KGB would know within a month. If he produced, he would automatically and irrevocably establish his bona fides. And if he produced, the Soviets would not care who he was; he could be a Ubangi riverboat captain, and they would make him admiral of the Soviet fleet if he gave crypto.

John Walker had worked with ciphers and cryptographic material for years. The navy had sent him to school to learn how to repair cipher machines. So he well understood what ciphers represented and all that was necessary to break them. And that is what he began methodically to collect for the KGB.

He flew from Norfolk to Washington in February 1968. In a locker at National Airport he put his first haul — key cards for the KWR-37, the next month's keylist for the KL-47, other Adonis system keys, and his duty schedule. A fifteen-minute cab ride took him to the rendezvous area, the parking lot of a Zayre department store.*

The sun had just set, and darkness rapidly descended as Walker roamed the parking lot, nervously holding a copy of *Time* magazine. An even more nervous man approached and asked, "Have you something for me?"

"I left it in an airport locker."

Near panic, the KGB officer exclaimed that security guards at any minute might open the locker. He drove Walker to the airport and waited outside. When Walker returned with film and documents, the KGB officer gave him a package and a Minox camera, then hastily departed in fright. It was not a textbook meeting, but it succeeded.

The package astonished Walker, and it might have intoxicated him had he been able to appreciate its full significance. It contained a tight roll of fifty-dollar bills totaling five thousand dollars; elaborate instructions minutely detailing drop

---

*Walker remembers that the Zayre store was in Arlington or Alexandria, Virginia. Probably it was located at the western edge of Alexandria on Little River Turnpike near Annandale.

and signal procedures; maps and photographs of sites; and a message. The instructions and message, neatly printed by hand in faultless English, amounted to an introductory course in espionage tradecraft. And they reflected decisions that could have been made only at the highest levels of the KGB, very likely with the personal approval of Chairman Yuri Andropov himself.

Normally, in developing an agent, the KGB uses money to control and condition, much as a scientist utilizes food and electric shock to condition rats in a laboratory maze. Desirable performance is rewarded with payments; unsatisfactory production or behavior is punished by withholding or reducing payments. Normally, in the development stage, the KGB does not make major payments before evaluating intelligence provided by the agent. Normally, within a reasonable time after recruitment, the KGB insists upon meeting the agent outside the United States so it can assess him personally and debrief him about all he knows.

But without waiting even to look at what Walker might bring to the February meeting, the Center decided to give him five thousand dollars — the equivalent in 1986 dollars of twelve thousand dollars and, at any time, a huge sum by Soviet standards. Rather than direct Walker to plan for an eventual meeting outside the country, the message informed him that there would be no more personal meetings except in the most desperate emergency. Communications would be effected through drops, the oldest, most basic and secure method in espionage. The KGB displayed no interest whatsoever in his wealth of knowledge about the capabilities, tactics, and operations of U.S. submarines.

In the first keylist he delivered, the Soviets had glimpsed a possibility of ultimately doing to the United States what the British and Americans had done to their enemies in World

War II by breaking ciphers. Now the Soviets subordinated everything to realization of that possibility.

Alone in a vault off the communications center in Norfolk, Walker with the Minox easily photographed cryptographic data and Top Secret messages. It was so easy that he thought, "K mart has better security than the navy."

Every few Saturdays, Walker drove or flew to Washington to make deliveries in the suburbs or nearby countryside. The loading and unloading of drops usually required him to go to six different sites within a general area. At the first site, he looked for a 7-Up can, whose presence signaled KGB readiness to proceed with the exchange. At the second, he left a 7-Up can to announce his readiness. At the third site, he deposited film, photocopies of documents, and sometimes original documents concealed at the bottom of a sack filled with trash. At the fourth site, he picked up the KGB package of money, instructions, and plans for the next exchange wrapped in heavy plastic. At the fifth site, he laid down another 7-Up can, which told the KGB he had picked up its package. At the last, he observed a 7-Up can denoting that the KGB had found his delivery. Absence of either of the first two signal cans aborted the exchange and automatically rescheduled it a week later. If Walker did not see the final signal can, he had to retrieve his package and try to deliver it the next week.

Although this routine was complicated, tedious, and time-consuming, Walker quickly mastered it, and through the years it never failed him or the Soviets. The KGB designated new sites for each exchange, and sometimes Walker had difficulty recognizing them because the photographs provided to him in advance had been taken at a different season. So he adopted the habit of reconnoitering a drop area in the afternoon prior to the nighttime exchange.

Walker exercised his own judgment and initiative in selecting data for the Soviets. Without being asked, he copied the technical manual that diagrammed the circuitry and logic of the KWR-37 cipher machine. With the manual, they could build their own copy of the KWR-37. Next he gave them KWR-37 key cards. To further facilitate their breaking into the system, he gave them plain-language texts of Top Secret messages, which could be compared with enciphered versions. And when the NSA introduced a new electronic insert, or secondary variable, into the KWR-37, he gave that away also. In sum, he supplied the KGB with everything needed to read all enciphered messages to and from American submarines as well as the bases and ships supporting them.

The volume and quality of cryptographic data flowing out of COMSUBLANT in the first months evidently overwhelmed the Soviets, for they reduced the frequency of exchanges to about one every three months and, in effect, ordered Walker to slow down. They also evinced new concern for his security. "If it's not safe, don't do it," a message commanded. He was to reach for nothing that was not within easy, natural, and safe grasp. Never should he try to recruit assistants or ferret information from others. In its first message back in February, the KGB advised Walker that he could request an emergency meeting in the United States by chalking the numeral 7 on a signal site in northern Virginia. Now it told him to forget about that; in no circumstances would a face-to-face meeting ever be attempted in the United States.

Walker had become too valuable to lose, too good to be true. But, as Soviet cryptanalysts tasked with penetration of American ciphers attested, all that he delivered was true.

Through 1968 and 1969 the operation progressed flawlessly. Walker continually purveyed key cards, keylists, and rotor readings for the KWR-37, KW-26, and Adonis systems, along with technical manuals and a choice selection of secret documents that came his way. He relished being a spy. Espionage set him apart from the plodding clods serving out their time around him; it was challenging and exciting; and it paid well. Heeding KGB admonishments, he avoided conspicuous cash expenditures and made installment purchases, spreading payments over a protracted period. Having become a spy, he thought he always must be one. And since he had embarked upon a new lifetime profession, he wanted to be very good at it.

In 1970 his production unavoidably shriveled after the navy transferred him to be director of the Practical Applications Laboratory at the communications school in San Diego. There simply was not much at the school to steal — some secret messages, monthly intelligence digests, some aircraft cryptographic material. Walker apologized for the relative meagerness of the hauls he brought to Washington area drops every six months or so. Still exploiting the immense take from the Norfolk bonanza, the KGB did not complain. It did reduce his payments to two thousand dollars a month.

While reiterating the stricture forbidding Walker to attempt any recruitments himself, the KGB asked him to try to spot personnel who might be approachable by other agents. In time, he fixed his attention on one of his subordinates, Jerry Alfred Whitworth.

Both men liked to sail, and during leisurely hours in Walker's boat *Dirty Old Man* off San Diego, they became friends of sorts. Walker appraised Whitworth as "a very sixty-ish person," a silent rebel bereft of any spiritual or philosophical moorings. Talking approvingly of the motion picture *Easy Rider,* Whitworth remarked, "You know, I could pull off a big-time crime just once if there was a big payoff." Whitworth confided that he had been married for a few months, then divorced, but that he had not informed the navy and continued to draw a marital allotment. Walker thought, "So he's larcenous." Whitworth defied navy regulations and smoked marijuana, signifying to Walker that he would take risks. Aware of Whitworth's attentions to the high school student from North Dakota, Walker thought there was something not quite right about a thirty-two-year-old man who seriously pursues a sixteen-year-old girl.

Yet Whitworth was a sound radioman with excellent technical knowledge and an unsullied record. Walker marked him down for the future. Of course, he said nothing to the Soviets about Whitworth. Why should he? If the KGB ever was to benefit from Whitworth, so would he.

To restore his production and payments to previous levels, Walker midway through his tour volunteered for sea duty, and in the summer of 1971 he was assigned to the USS *Niagara Falls*. Whether he finagled this particular assignment or received it by chance is unclear. But if the KGB had been accorded the option of putting a spy anywhere it desired in the U.S. armed forces, it could not have picked a billet better than the one Walker obtained.

The *Niagara Falls* was a fast, modern supply ship, a kind of floating grocery store and warehouse from which warships replenished at sea. Ranging far and wide across the Pacific into both eastern and western theaters, the *Niagara Falls* had to be able to communicate with all types of ships and to know their operational plans. Thus, it carried a variety of cipher machines — the KW-7, KY-8, KG-14, KWR-37, and KL-47 — as well as the technical manuals and at least ninety days of keying material for each. Sometimes it had on board key cards or lists for advance periods of more than ninety days.

From the day he arrived on the *Niagara Falls* until the day he departed three years later, in 1974, John Walker was its Communications Material Systems (CMS) custodian — guardian of all those cryptographic materials. He was responsible for receiving and inventorying them; for keeping them securely in a vault inside the CMS custodian's office, to which only he and an alternate custodian had keys; for dispensing materials as needed and destroying them once used. As the loss or mishandling of cryptographic data can result in an adverse fitness report, a reprimand, or worse, no one in the navy wants to trifle with crypto unless duty demands. The alternate custodian was appointed to fill in only in case Walker was on leave or incapacitated, and he rarely came around. The CMS custodian's office became Walker's private sanctuary and domain. He could sequester himself there with his Minox at any and all hours and photograph endlessly, completely secure from interruption.

Walker suffered only one concern. Anyone holding Top Secret or Crypto clearances is supposed to be reinvestigated every five years. Now shortages of funds and investigators, indifference toward security, and general incompetence have made a mockery of this once inviolate rule, and even in those days the reinvestigations that were made often were perfunctory. But Walker did not know this, and he was due for reinvestigation in 1971. His wife had told Arthur Walker and perhaps others that he was a spy, and he feared that investigators might hear rumors and consequently talk to her.

Walker disposed of the matter by forging a salmon-colored copy of the standard background investigation form, stamping it with a seal he had made for $2.98, and inserting it in his service record. The form showed that he had been reinvestigated in 1971 and no derogatory information discovered.

Two or three times a year when he could take leave, Walker flew to Washington to fill drops with the equivalent of pure gold for Soviet cryptanalysts. The copies of the technical manuals enabled their engineers to build copies of the cipher machines — machines used not only by the navy but by all the armed forces, the State Department, CIA, and FBI. The Soviet versions may have looked different, but the logic, cir-

cuitry, and functions would be the same as the American versions. Together with the duplicated machines, the key cards, lists, and inserts for roughly twelve hundred days supplied by Walker enabled the Soviets to read enciphered naval messages just as easily as could their recipients on American carriers, submarines, and missile cruisers, or at the Pentagon, Pearl Harbor, or anywhere else. Unless Walker had given them advance keys so they could break on the same day messages were transmitted, they had to wait until particular transmissions could be located and retrieved from the tapes on which all U.S. transmissions are recorded. But in peacetime, a few days' or weeks' delay did not make that much difference.

Because the keys for other services and agencies are different from those of the navy, the Soviets in theory could not break non-navy communications solely from Walker's gifts. But these gifts advanced by light-years the theoretical assault upon all American systems.

Usually with his deliveries of cryptographic data Walker threw in deciphered copies of secret messages. He did so to revalidate his access, importance, and reliability in Soviet eyes; to expedite the Soviets' entry into American ciphers by allowing them to compare enciphered and plain-language texts; and to give them something sent in a system possibly unbroken.

The KGB manifested no particular interest in this ancillary material until Walker included the operational plan for a fleet exercise together with its communications annex. This greatly excited the Soviets, and understandably. By showing precisely how the U.S. Navy organized and deployed itself for battle, the operational plan gave them priceless lessons in the tactics of a modern oceangoing fleet, which they were in the process of building. The communications annex, specifying which radio frequencies would be used for various purposes, told them where to listen for what. A KGB message Walker picked up at the next drop asked for more OpPlans.

In late summer 1974 Walker received orders transferring him from the *Niagara Falls* back to staff duty in Norfolk. Shipmates were sorry to see him go. Alan Cusick, now a successful attorney in San Francisco, who was an ensign when Walker was on the ship, recalls: "He was very witty and always in good humor. He was generous and helpful in teaching young officers the ways of the navy and how to deal with the men. I remember one weekend I had to put my car in the garage for repairs. He insisted on lending me his. Everybody liked him." Walker left the *Niagara Falls* with a highly laudatory fitness report, which particularly commended his performance as custodian of cryptographic materials.

Walker was uncertain about how much access he could obtain in Norfolk. Looking ahead, he feared the reinvestigation of his background due in 1976, and he ruled out another forgery as too dangerous. Concluding he would have to leave the navy in a couple of years to avoid investigation, he thought about how he could continue in espionage.

In late summer or early fall he visited Whitworth, who now was out of the navy and contemplating school in San Diego. Sitting at a back table in Boom Trenchard's Flare Path restaurant, Walker began, "There's something I'd like to discuss with you. But first, you must swear that you'll never tell anybody about it."

"Sure," Whitworth replied.

"I have a market for classified military information," Walker announced. "I've been selling it for some time, and there's a lot of money in it."

Whitworth appeared shocked, amazed. Then he smiled. And Walker sensed he had him. He hinted there were multiple buyers — the Mafia, the Israelis, publications, private research organizations. The problem was that he had to leave the navy in a year or two. If Whitworth would reenter the navy and supply cryptographic and communications data, Walker would deliver it to the buyers and split the profits. They each could make "a couple of thousand a month, maybe a lot more."

Whitworth gave Walker another crooked smile. "How long have you been doing this?"

"Long enough to know that it's easy, that there's little chance of getting caught."

Like Chester Nimitz and Janet Fournier, who came from tiny Texas towns culturally the same as Muldrow, Oklahoma, like countless other youths who dreamed of where the train heard in the night might take them, Jerry Whitworth always wanted to do something of note, to be somebody. In quest of distinction, Whitworth, the plain farmboy who harvested soybeans, the high school class clown, often pretended to be what he was not. Now, at age thirty-four, anonymously adrift and jobless, he perceived in Walker's proposition an opportunity truly to distinguish himself. Whitworth also construed Walker's willingness to trust him with such dangerous knowledge as a manifestation of real friendship. Having never had a real friend, he was heartened to discover one. As Walker had calculated he would, Whitworth agreed to the partnership in espionage.

The U.S. Navy, which pioneered satellite communications, was introducing them into the fleet, and their evolution obviously would interest the "buyers." So in reenlisting, Whitworth negotiated to attend the satellite communications school at Fort Monmouth, New Jersey, and to spend another year on Diego Garcia, where he would have wide access to cryptographic material. The navy was happy to find a qualified volunteer for this lonely hardship outpost, and Whitworth professed to be happy that he again could indulge his passion for scuba diving in the Indian Ocean.

After completing the course in New Jersey, Whitworth in February 1975 stopped in Norfolk to give Walker a navy satellite communications manual and other materials from the school. Walker advanced him four thousand dollars from his own funds and supplied him with Minox film. They agreed to a crude code in which "dive" meant theft of secret material and "photographic equipment" signified the material itself.

While Whitworth settled in on Diego Garcia, Walker became the CMS custodian of cryptographic materials on the staff of the commander of Atlantic surface forces. The data available at the staff command were not as extensive as on the *Niagara Falls,* and he had to be much more cautious in making copies. Nevertheless, he was able to unveil for the Soviets yet another cipher system, the KY-3, together with all its keys for more than a year. Additionally, he provided numerous OpPlans and Top Secret messages.

On Diego Garcia, Whitworth also eventually became CMS custodian, and in a letter dated June 28, 1975, he signaled Walker: "I finally made my first dive, it was real good." At the end of his tour on the island in March 1976, Whitworth took sixty days leave and flew to Norfolk. He brought a hoard of film completely compromising three cipher systems by showing their technical manuals, keys, and secret messages sent through them. The loot indeed was "real good," so good that Walker paid Whitworth eighteen thousand dollars of his own money.

Whitworth was proud of his accomplishment, the money, and the approbation Walker bestowed upon him. At last he was somebody. He vacationed in the Caribbean, took Brenda Reis from North Dakota to Las Vegas and married her there, then reported for duty aboard the USS *Constellation,* a carrier based in Bremerton, Washington. His job included supervision of cryptographic operations.

Sure that he could count upon and manipulate Whitworth

as a source, Walker in a message left at a northern Virginia drop broke the news to the KGB: because of his inability to survive an impending background investigation, he had no choice except to retire from the navy in July. However, he had been fortunate enough to recruit as his personal agent a reliable friend, Jerry Alfred Whitworth, who could sustain the flow of quality cryptographic and communications data. The new arrangement necessitated that the Soviets double their payments. With the message he included the film from Diego Garcia, emphasizing that Whitworth was the procurer.

Walker retired from the navy in July 1976 as announced. In August he made a quick trip to San Diego to pick up Whitworth's first take from the *Constellation* preparatory to filling a drop in September. Whitworth now was performing so well that he was about to be promoted to chief petty officer, and the crypto material passed on film was excellent.

The KGB angrily berated Walker in the message deposited at the next drop. He had flagrantly and irresponsibly defied orders by recruiting Whitworth. He had jeopardized himself and the whole operation. Who the hell was Whitworth? Where was he? What was he doing? How much did he know? The message also advised that since Walker was out of the navy and free to travel, the KGB wanted to meet him personally overseas.

The rebuke troubled Walker not at all. Through Whitworth, he still was supplying the Soviets with fresh cryptographic material just as valuable as before. Did the assholes want it or not? They did, and the KGB package included money for Whitworth.

Whitworth delivered more from the *Constellation* in January and April of 1977. In exchange for these deliveries, Walker received through a drop in April explicit instructions for a clandestine rendezvous with the KGB in Casablanca the coming August. Since the *Constellation* was scheduled to

176

dock in Hong Kong in early August, Walker by correspondence arranged to meet Whitworth there prior to the Casablanca rendezvous.

On film secreted in ten emptied cigarette packages and several Q-Tips boxes, Whitworth brought real treasures to the Holiday Inn in Hong Kong. They included the communications plans for naval forces operating throughout the Pacific; technical manuals diagramming the KW-7 and KWR-37 cipher systems, along with a new one, the KY-36. The navy had perfected a system, the KY-8, that allowed an admiral at sea to speak securely to the chief of naval operations or even the president in Washington. The film passed in Hong Kong also bared that system. Additionally, it provided keys and thousands of messages enciphered in these systems. Walker gave Whitworth eight thousand dollars, raising the total of payments to him thus far in 1977 to twenty-eight thousand dollars.

Because the *Constellation* had arrived late in Hong Kong, Walker missed the first scheduled meeting in Casablanca and had to attempt the rendezvous on the alternate day one week later. In the early evening, he directed a taxi driver to what he understood to be a residential area of Casablanca. The driver in broken English warned that the area was dangerous at night and a foreigner should not venture into it. Walker ordered him to drive on. At a point designated by the KGB instructions, he got out and began walking along a tortuous route they prescribed, making at least eight turns through narrow, dark Moroccan streets. He carried a magazine in his left hand and felt like a scared fool.

The KGB representative was supposed to identify himself by asking, "Excuse me, didn't I meet you in Berlin in 1976?" Walker was to identify himself by replying, "No, I was in Norfolk, Virginia, during that hectic year."

Instead, as Walker stood at an intersection, a voice said,

"Welcome, friend. We have worried about you. We have been hysterical."

Walker estimated that the Russian was about six feet tall and in his mid-thirties. He had dark hair, a swarthy complexion, and a clean-shaven, pleasant face. Walker was sure his eyeglasses were fake, worn only to mislead. Despite a thick accent, he spoke English well. "Do you have something?" he asked.

Walker handed over the package of Whitworth's film, which the Russian clasped tightly to his side as they walked and talked for about an hour. "Why do you come so late?"

Without apologizing, Walker explained that the *Constellation* was delayed in reaching Hong Kong. It would have been pointless to fly on without Whitworth's film.

The KGB officer began to remonstrate about the unauthorized recruitment of Whitworth, but Walker cut him short. "I had no choice. I know Jerry; I knew what I was doing. Look at his stuff. It's goddamned good."

"It is. But we are concerned first of all about your security. You could have been arrested."

"I wasn't. We've worked together now almost three years. The setup is perfect."

"We all have been fortunate. Please do not do it again. Consult us first. We want to help you. We have experience in these matters."

Walker shrugged as if to say, "So do I."

At the officer's insistence, Walker recited Whitworth's background, marital status, and access and prospects in the navy; as objectively as he could, he assessed his character, ideology, and motivation. The Russian seemed satisfied. He was even more satisfied when Walker outlined the content of the film.

Walker also was questioned about his own personal circumstances and prospects. The KGB officer thought the work as a private detective would afford superb cover and help hide clandestine income. He regretted Walker's divorce but accepted that Walker probably would be more secure separated than with his wife.

Although its concern was not entirely altruistic, the KGB remained genuinely apprehensive about the safety of Walker and now Whitworth. They were not to take chances, the KGB reiterated. "If it's not safe, don't do it." They were to take only what came their way. Conspicuous spending could be their undoing.

As for collection requirements, cryptographic data and especially any pertaining to new systems remained the highest priority. Operational communications plans were very much desired. Top Secret message traffic was all right if obtained without risk. Intelligence messages and summaries were really not that important in comparison to crypto. In no circumstances should they attempt to ferret military or any other secrets outside the realm of communications.

Somewhat to Walker's surprise, the KGB at this, its first opportunity to talk to him directly since 1968, asked him nothing about submarines. He could have told a lot. But if they didn't want to know, he figured that was the problem of those dumb shits. Then he thought maybe they weren't so dumb. Maybe they didn't need to ask; maybe crypto was telling them what they needed to know.

The KGB officer made a few hesitant gestures toward flattering Walker about his contributions to peace and in an uncertain way tried to build personal rapport. Perhaps sensing that he was confronted by a character not easily charmed, he did not press. Nor, having been curtly rebuffed when he attempted censure about the recruitment of Whitworth, did he try to intimidate.

Rather, he asked if henceforth Walker could travel abroad once or twice a year for personal meetings, and if so, did

179

he prefer any particular country? Walker said he could travel, and he did not care where; he expected compensation for travel expenses, including those incurred in meeting Whitworth.

"Would you like India?"

"India! I'll go wherever you want. But why the hell India, of all places, for Christ's sake?"

"Okay, okay. It will be Vienna." He gave Walker a packet containing thirty-five thousand or forty-five thousand dollars (Walker is not sure) and inordinately complex instructions for a January 1978 rendezvous, typed under the title "The Vienna Procedure."

Crossing the Atlantic on the last stage of his journey around the world, Walker mused: "They wanted me in Vienna all the time. That poor jailed son of a bitch just wanted to sightsee in some exotic place like India. Come to think of it, like Casablanca. Why Casablanca?"

Walker may have been on the mark. The officer doubtless was permanently stationed in Moscow with Department 16, and his opportunities to enjoy foreign travel would be scant. Had Walker said, "Sure, India is fine," he could have reported India as Walker's choice and gotten himself a trip to New Delhi or Bombay.

Whitworth took leave the last week in November 1977 to give crypto data from the *Constellation* to Walker in San Diego. The take again was outstanding.

In January 1978 Walker flew with it to Milan, then boarded a train for Vienna. En route, he studied "The Vienna Procedure" he would have to follow. The instructions said:

At 1815 p.m. come to the "Komet Kuechen" store (kitchen cabinets and appliants) on the corner of Schoenbrunner Strasse and Ruckergasse. To get there, walk from Schoenbrunn Palace and Park Grounds on Schoenbrunner Schlosstrasse and its continuation Schoenbrunner Strasse to Ruckergasse. Turn left on the latter and stop at the window of the "Komet Kuechen" store, which is looking on Ruckergasse, just a couple of yards away from the corner. For easy identification, please carry your camera bag on your left shoulder and hold a small paper bag in your right hand.

Pause by that window for about two minutes from 1815 p.m. to 1817 p.m., drifting slowly along it away from Schoenbrunner Strasse toward the other corner of the building. Then turn around the corner on Fabrikgasse. Walk a few yards on it, then come back on Ruckergasse, walk to Schoenbrunner Strasse, cross it, walk a few yards on Ruckergasse past the pillars supporting the overhanging second floor at the corner of the "Fernsehkratky" store (selling TV sets, stereo systems, etc.). The window in question is the right one after the last pillar and has a vertical sign "Fernsehkratky" to its right. Then continue one block on Ruckergasse, right and one block on Nymphengasse, left and two blocks on Ehrenfelgasse and left again on Haschkagasse. (The street sign at this corner is pretty old and barely readable.) Walk one block on Haschkagasse to Ruckergasse, cross it and continue along a narrow pedestrian lane Fuechselhofgasse which widens to a regular street halfway through it. Walk on it to Meidunger Hauptstrasse, cross to the other side of the latter, turn left and continue on to the right-hand side of this street. Past a small square on your left to Schoenbrunner Strasse. You'll see a Stadtbahn Station. Cross it when reaching this intersection. Turn around and walk back one block on Meidunger Hauptstrasse, then left and one block on Neiderhof Strasse, right and one block Vivenotgasse, right and one block on Reschgasse to Meidunger Hauptstrasse. Turn right onto the latter, pause briefly by the windows of the two ladies' apparel stores which are near this corner, then cross Reschgasse and walk two blocks uphill on Meidunger Hauptstrasse to Bonygasse. Turn left on the latter, walk two blocks to its end, then right and two blocks on Ignazgasse, left and two blocks on Rauchgasse to Vierthalergasse. Turn left onto it and stroll one block downhill. Then turn left on Kirchbaum-gasse; walk two blocks to Reschgasse. Turn left on it and stroll one block to Meidunger Hauptstrasse. Then left and one block down Fuechselhofgasse. It should take you about 40 minutes to negotiate this route. When moving along it, pause occasionally by the store windows. At 1855 p.m. stop at the men's apparel store "Bazala Internationale Kleidung" on the corner of Meidunger Hauptstrasse and Fuechselhofgasse. Browse around its window displays inside short passages in the corner section of this building from 1855 to 1858 p.m. You'll be contacted either at the "Bazala" store or somewhere on your route. If no one contacts you, please use alternate dates and the same route.

On the night of January 21, Walker set out in a blizzard to follow the crazy-quilt route. The streets soon emptied as everyone with any sense took refuge from the snow and ice. Leaning into the wind, Walker struggled on until about 7:00 P.M., when he reached the men's store at the end and found some shelter in an arcade.

"Greetings, friend," said the same KGB officer who had met him in Casablanca. "Have you something?"

Taking from Walker the package of Whitworth's film, he whispered, "Wait here. I will come back soon."

Walker looked forward to the warmth of one of those safe houses about which he had read in spy novels and perhaps a fire and brandy; at the least, he expected a schnitzel and beer in a little café. That was not to be. Returning after about ten minutes, the KGB officer announced they would walk and talk as in Casablanca. Walker thought, "Can't you see there's a goddamned blizzard, you asshole?" But he said nothing and trailed along.

As if reciting a catechism, the Soviet asked questions and repeated admonitions about security. Where does Jerry (as he now called him) photograph the keys, manuals, and messages? On ship, or does he take them home? Where does he hide the film? Where do you meet? What is he doing with the money? Does he drink too much? Take drugs? How do you justify your travels? Your meetings with Jerry?

Because the KGB officer had no concept of navy life or shipboard routine, Walker had difficulty explaining. But he managed to convey that Whitworth's position afforded him constant access to crypto and communications material and abundant opportunity to photograph it secure on ship. Whitworth had taken the precaution of letting everyone know that he was an avid photographer. Removal and subsequent concealment of the small rolls of Minox film were simple matters.

As a detective, Walker naturally had to travel, and he had dropped word here and there that he was exploring business interests on the West Coast. Naturally, if business gave him the chance, he would chat a few hours with an old navy buddy. They exchanged film and money in the seclusion of motel rooms and talked outside beyond the reach of bugs.

Next, the KGB officer endeavored to influence Walker ideologically by talking about peace and the Soviet Union. "In the West, my country is much misunderstood. The Soviet Union is twice as big as the United States. In Siberia we have much minerals. We do not need other territory. We do not want to rule the world. We only want peace. The imperialists always threaten war."

Walker kept wondering when he would come to the point of the meeting. As it turned out, there was no point, or none discernible to Walker. After whispering in the wind, snow, and sleet for about forty minutes, the officer scheduled a July meeting in Vienna, gave Walker a packet with instructions and money, and bade him good luck.

Back at the small Viennese hotel where the KGB commanded him to stay, Walker, the only American around, asked himself what had been accomplished that could not have been accomplished through a drop. Nothing. "Those assholes. They're so screwed up. They make everything so complicated. And that Mother Russia bullshit! Jesus!"

A couple of weeks after returning to Norfolk, Walker, who had taken up flying, flew in his private plane to San Diego, gave Whitworth ten thousand dollars in back pay for the previous five months, and picked up more crypto from the *Constellation*. Without incident, he left it in a drop March 11. A KGB message congratulated him and Whitworth upon the excellence of their production and noted an increase in their pay.

In another San Diego meeting on July 7, Walker gave Whitworth twenty-four thousand dollars, representing a 50 percent jump in pay. He received what was to be the last load from the *Constellation*. For Whitworth had just been detached to join another ship.

On July 15 Walker, following the same devious route as in January, kept the scheduled appointment with his KGB case officer in Vienna. Just as before, the officer first took the film and excused himself for ten to fifteen minutes, then led Walker on a stroll. As before, he asked about Whitworth.

"He's been transferred," Walker announced.

The Soviet reacted as if Walker had slugged him in the stomach. "Where?"

"The *Niagara Falls*. My old ship. He has the same job I had."

Slowly the KGB officer comprehended the momentous meaning. "Exactly the same?"

"Yep. CMS custodian."

"That's wonderful."

"It should be."

Whitworth reported aboard the *Niagara Falls* August 10, 1978, and assumed control of all its diverse cipher machines and materials. Locked in the same office Walker occupied from 1971 to 1974, he began photographing furiously, eliciting

184

approval from superiors and sneers from a few subordinates for his single-minded dedication to duty. His Minox was to open a new wealth of American cryptographic secrets to the KGB. The latest technical manuals were photographed, laying bare recent modifications and any new secondary variables introduced into the most commonly used U.S. machines. Advance keys permitted the Soviets to read enciphered U.S. messages in "real time," or at the same time American recipients read them.

On September 18, little more than five weeks after he went aboard, Whitworth took leave from the ship while it was moored in Oakland and passed to Walker a mass of film. The KGB retrieved it from a drop outside Washington on November 18.

The *Niagara Falls* now sailed on a prolonged expedition that took it into both the western and eastern theaters of the Pacific. Because of Whitworth's extraordinary access, Walker arranged to meet him in Manila on December 15 when the ship put into port there.

That night in Walker's room at the Philippine Plaza, Whitworth made the most "tremendous" single delivery of his espionage career. It included the latest complete diagrams of the KW-7, KY-8, KG-14, KWR-37, and KL-47 cipher machines, together with all the keys for fleets deployed in both the eastern and western Pacific. The Soviets scarcely could have asked for more. The data were so comprehensively revealing that Walker in the morning immediately flew back to the United States to hide the film. In another blizzard, he turned it over to the same KGB officer in Vienna on January 27, 1979.

For reasons unclear, Whitworth had kept his 1976 marriage in Las Vegas to young Brenda secret. On their third wedding anniversary, in May 1979, he hosted a lavish party at the grand old Hotel Del Coronado in San Diego to announce and celebrate the marriage. Walker flew out to attend and to take delivery of more precious film shot in the vault on the *Niagara Falls*. He met a very pretty girl who intimated readiness to enjoy an amorous weekend with him. Because of the film, he had to turn her down.

Walker handed the film to the same KGB officer during another Vienna street meeting June 30, 1979. By now the officer was comfortable with him and tried to be friendly.

Without implying that it was anybody's fault, he reported that a major difficulty had developed. "The KWR-37 has stopped breaking. With other systems, there is no problem. But KWR-37 won't break anymore."*

Walker honestly said he did not know why and he would consult Whitworth.

"No, do not tell him. Just ask him to try to get more about KWR-37."

Despite difficulties with this one system, Whitworth's performance and the whole operation elated the KGB. In all solemnity, the case officer confided that in recognition of Walker's outstanding contribution to peace, he had been awarded the rank of admiral in the Soviet navy. Keeping a straight face, Walker said, "Tell them thanks a lot."

Walker appreciated that the title of admiral of the Soviet navy would not be all that useful to him in Norfolk. He also appreciated that as an espionage middleman, or principal agent, he was entirely dependent upon the performance and survival of a lone supplier, Whitworth. He had begun to think about how he could secure his future by augmenting his sources.

In the standard review of his personal circumstances, he mentioned that his daughter Laura was entering the army to be a communications specialist. He suggested that under his

---

*While Walker thinks the announcement of difficulty with the KWR-37 was made at this meeting, he is not sure. The KGB may have disclosed the trouble earlier.

paternal tutelage she could be developed into a first-rate agent who carries on for decades in the communications field. Then there was brother Arthur, a retired submarine officer employed by a firm that did extensive consultant work for the navy. Though he did not have sensational access at the moment, he could be brought along.

Incredulous, the KGB officer ruled out both prospective recruitments as too perilous; the daughter or brother might inform the authorities; the addition of either as an agent would multiply the risks disproportionately to what either could contribute.

Though Walker did not so inform the KGB, he knew that his former wife habitually had told his children that he was a spy. On the street in Vienna, he put it a little differently. He could conceal his large illicit income from outsiders, but not from his immediate family. Laura and Arthur had to know he was involved in something very illegal, yet they never had incriminated him. They never would; they were of the same flesh and blood. As for operational risks, they hardly could be less. What could be more natural than father talking to daughter, brother to brother?

Noncommittally, the KGB officer questioned him closely about Laura and Arthur, then said, "We will see."

When Whitworth went aboard the *Niagara Falls,* he expected to serve a normal tour of three years, and Walker so advised the KGB. Understandably and gleefully, the Soviets thus anticipated virtually unrestricted access to navy ciphers for the next three years. However, in the summer of 1979, Whitworth learned that the *Niagara Falls* was going into dry dock for extensive overhaul and renovation that would keep it out of service for many months, perhaps a year. While it was in dry dock, all cipher machines and crypto material would be removed to shore for safekeeping, as there would be no need for them on the ship. Whitworth would be able to steal nothing at all.

With Walker's concurrence, Whitworth, who was overdue for shore duty, requested and received an assignment to the Naval Telecommunications Center at Alameda, California. Immediately after leaving the *Niagara Falls* on August 10, 1979, he went to Norfolk with the last yield from that bonanza.

In his original, cold assessments of Whitworth as a prospective spy, Walker discerned one troubling defect, an apparently irreversible tendency to vacillate. He had joined the navy, left to try school, given that up, gone back into the navy, left again to try school, given up again, and returned to the navy. He never seemed to know for very long what he wanted to do.

But ever since Walker hooked him, he had been steadfast, and espionage had become the purpose of his life. In Norfolk, Whitworth remarked, "Doesn't it bother you that we both will probably die without anybody knowing how good we were?" And he mentioned that he was considering divorcing his wife so that, unencumbered, he could devote himself wholly to spying. Though disappointed by the premature end of his tour on the *Niagara Falls,* he was confident about what he could do at Alameda, one of the navy's major communications bases, which could relay messages anywhere in the world.

In early September, Walker left the final film from the *Niagara Falls* at a drop, together with a message explaining Whitworth's transfer.

At Alameda, Whitworth did enjoy exceptional access. In addition to being CMS custodian, he was chief of the Message Center and managed the Autodin Center, which linked navy, army, and air force bases throughout the world. But there was a problem. Alameda was a bustling operational communications center, manned by a large watch around the clock. While Whitworth could enter the safes at any time, people almost always were nearby, and photography was dangerous. He could slip a few documents out at night in his briefcase and plead oversight if caught. He dared not take key material out, for nothing could justify its possession outside the center. When Walker visited him at his home in San Leandro, California, on January 19, 1980, before flying to Vienna, Whitworth had comparatively little to offer. Understanding, Walker recommended that he buy a van, outfit it for photography, and take shots on the base during lunch hour.

Five days later in Vienna amid more howling winter winds, the KGB officer, without the customary fraternal greeting, performed the ritual of grabbing Walker's package and disappearing. Returning, he spoke to Walker in an accusatory tone. "Why did Jerry leave his ship?"

"I told you in the exchange."

"You told three years. You told he would be on ship three years."

"I didn't know it was going into dry dock."

"Why did it go there?"

"Goddammit, I don't run the U.S. Navy. How the hell would I know? Obviously, somebody thought it needed repairs."

"Why did Jerry leave?"

Walker shouted in the night. "You dumb asshole, he lost his fucking access! I explained that. Am I dealing with idiots?"

Probably realizing he was losing control, the KGB officer conciliated. "My friend, there is misunderstanding. Please explain to me so I can make them understand."

Walker repressed his exasperation and, event by event, explained the causes and consequences of all that had transpired. He concluded by emphasizing that, far from being derelict or duplicitous, Whitworth had made the best of adversity and insinuated himself into a billet affording access nearly as good as that aboard the *Niagara Falls*. He further explained the problem of photographing at Alameda and how they proposed to overcome it by purchasing a van.

The explanation convinced and relieved the KGB officer, so much so that he agreed the KGB should pay ten thousand dollars toward purchase of the van. As if to demonstrate that all now was well, he suggested that they duck into a café for coffee.

Because of intensifying security at European and American airports, the Russian explained, the KGB worried about Walker carrying large sums of cash on his person. Therefore, it intended to transmit major sums through drops in the future. Walker, who would have preferred to conduct all business through drops, quickly agreed.

Toward the end of the conversation, the Russian authorized Walker to sound out Laura and Arthur and assess how they were likely to react to an actual recruitment approach.

Evidently, Walker's accounting at Vienna completely satisfied the Center in Moscow. For on May 18, 1980, the KGB left more than $200,000 for him in a woods outside Washington.

On May 30 Walker and a girlfriend landed in California to be greeted by Whitworth and his wife. In a new customized van, they sipped champagne and ate rare cheese around a table lit by candles as they drove to San Leandro. Alone with Whitworth the next day, Walker presented him with $100,000 in $50 bills. Clutching the cash, Whitworth danced a little jig and giggled. "I've never held a hundred thousand dollars before."

The van, he reported, neatly solved the problem. Letting it be known that his physician had put him on a new health regimen requiring exercise and a noontime nap, he daily repaired to the van parked outside the telecommunications center. He regularly ordered subordinates to be sure to come out and awaken him if he overslept and failed to return by 1:00 P.M. Curtains drawn, he rapidly photographed documents and key material inside the locked van. He hoped to provide an unbroken chain of cipher system keys for the months ahead.

In ways, Whitworth exceeded his goals. On November 6, 1980, he took leave to fly to Norfolk with accumulated film constituting one of his most spectacular deliveries. It contained copies of the technical manual and keys for a new cipher system, the KG-36; the technical manual and keys for the KWR-37, which should solve the Soviets' difficulties with that system; the first breakthrough into Autodin and its KW-26 cipher system; and ninety straight days of keys for other systems.

Three weeks later, on a cold, rainy night in Vienna, Walker slipped the film to his KGB handler and outlined the contents. The Soviet was jubilant. "Tell him we give ten-thousand-dollar bonus every time he give ninety days' keys."

On June 6, 1981, the KGB deposited $100,000 in a drop outside Washington along with a message commending Whitworth. On July 12 Walker gave $50,000 to Whitworth, who visited him in Norfolk.

On the night of February 13, 1982, when Walker rendezvoused in Vienna with more film from Alameda, his handler brought along another KGB officer whom he introduced as his successor. He was a stocky, swarthy man about forty years old with a large head and a wide, flat, impassive face. Walker thought, "A Russian heavy straight out of central casting."

The first officer seemed genuinely saddened by the necessity of saying farewell. He recalled their meetings since Casablanca and expressed regret that they would not meet again. "Spy business is not easy business. You do it well." As a memento of their association, he gave Walker a red Paper Mate ballpoint pen. To emphasize its value, he said he bought it at a special hard-currency store in Moscow.

At a drop on June 13, Walker received in excess of $120,000, and on September 28 at Whitworth's home in San Leandro, he gave him $60,000. Whitworth was about to depart for duty aboard the nuclear aircraft carrier *Enterprise*. And Walker sensed that his dedication to espionage was diminishing.

A security breach at Alameda had precipitated an investigation by swarms of inspectors. Whitworth was neither involved nor implicated. Coincidentally, he was transferred on temporary additional duty to Stockton, California, for three months to help install a new communications system. Upon returning to Alameda, he resumed copying crypto material. But the investigation may have frightened him.

In any case, he reverted to his old talk about retiring from the navy, which in effect meant retiring from espionage, and schooling himself to be a stockbroker or computer salesman or something; he did not know what. He had retrogressed into vacillation.

"Look, Jerry, this is big-time international espionage," Walker told him. "You don't just walk out. Who do you think we're dealing with, some little guy in western New York?" Whitworth said he understood. But Walker now doubted him.

Aboard the *Enterprise* as technical control chief, Whitworth had access to the most secret messages in the U.S. Navy as well as to keys and other materials pertaining to the KW-7, KG-14, KG-36, KWR-37, KY-3, and KY-57 cipher systems. Just before going aboard on October 11, 1982, he bought a huge supply of Minox film. And a fellow sailor, Ronald Meyers, recalls seeing classified documents in his locker after they put to sea.

Because of the carrier's operational schedule, Walker was

unable to deliver any film from the *Enterprise* when he met his new handler in Vienna on January 15, 1983. He did bring the last film Whitworth shot at Alameda, a very respectable take by any standards.

Always, Walker was scrupulously honest in whatever he told or wrote to the KGB. He did not let them know everything; what he did say was accurate. He intended to inform the KGB of Whitworth's disturbing talk about retirement, objectively analyze his vacillation, then propose a solution. He felt the KGB could lock Whitworth in permanently by guaranteeing him $100,000 a year if he remained in the navy and produced another ten years.

But before Walker could broach the problem, he fell under assault from his new handler. The officer insinuated that Whitworth was responsible for the security breach at Alameda and denounced him for producing little while at Stockton, where there was little to steal. Then he resurrected the dead issue of Whitworth's premature departure from the *Niagara Falls*. He even denounced Walker for his late arrival in Casablanca years ago.

Struggling through the snow en route to the meeting, Walker had thought, "I'm tired of wandering around the streets in blizzards like a goddamned hobo. I'll buy these bastards some books by John le Carré so they can learn how to run a spy operation."

Given his mood, the KGB officer's outburst was too much.

"You stupid bastards," Walker exploded. "You tell us to play it safe. 'If it's not safe, don't do it.' If you've said it once, you've said it a hundred times. Then we have every fucking inspector in the world crawling all over the place, and you expect us to go in and photograph before their eyes. At Stockton he had no access, no fucking access. Do you understand what that means? You assholes, read what I wrote."

The Department 16 officer, who probably never had handled an agent abroad before, recoiled and apologized. However, in view of the irrational KGB suspicions, Walker thought the time not right to warn of the possibility that Whitworth might retire and to propose preventive action. The meeting ended with neither party fully mollified.

After the *Enterprise* sailed into San Francisco (and got stuck on a sandbar in the process), Walker on June 3 obtained from Whitworth in San Leandro copies of numerous documents bearing Top Secret and higher classifications and a large quantity of film. Nine days later, he delivered all to the KGB through a drop in the Washington area. Although this first take from the *Enterprise* was excellent, Whitworth's continuing vagueness about his future plans troubled Walker. He felt an acute need to protect himself with another source. So he turned to his son, Michael, who largely at his behest had joined the navy.

In retrospect, Michael believes his father long groomed him for espionage.

By the summer of 1980, Michael had dropped out of school, was using drugs, and was having trouble with his alcoholic mother, with whom he lived in Maine. His parents agreed that he should be placed under his father's care in Norfolk. He then was sixteen.

Walker made Michael feel wanted and important by enrolling him in a private school, putting him in charge of the household, giving him at least one hundred dollars a week to administer it, and letting him work as a "partner" in his detective firm. One night while Michael still was in high school, Walker took him to a bar and remarked, "Someday I'll tell you how I make my money."

Like his sister Laura, Michael even as a child realized that his family had a dark secret and that his father derived income from some mysterious, probably illegal source. Several times while she was drinking, his mother had told him that his father was a "traitor" or involved with the Soviets. He dismissed these allegations as alcoholic hallucinations and guessed that his father was in some way engaged in narcotics traffic.

Michael excelled as a detective, or at least Walker assured him that he did. He very much liked snooping, investigating domestic relations and insurance cases. At night he took criminology courses at a community college, and upon turning eighteen he obtained a private detective license. Walker also secured for him a permit to carry a pistol.

However, Michael fared poorly in high school and barely managed to graduate. Though he hoped to go to college, Old Dominion University rejected him because of his low grades and Scholastic Aptitude Test scores.

The realization that he could not gain admission to a first-rate school prompted his decision to join the navy in December 1982. While the decision was his, Walker encouraged him. In the navy, he declared, Michael could demonstrate to his sisters that he could succeed at something — such as communications.

Michael in the summer of 1983 served in the administrative office of a fighter squadron then based in the Norfolk area. He mentioned to Walker that his duties entailed processing incoming registered mail, which included secret documents. Walker observed that depending upon his future assignments, Michael might be able to see a lot more classified information.

On a July evening while watching television, John Walker, without any introduction of the subject, said to his son, "You know, you could make a lot of money by obtaining classified material and giving it to me."

"Is that how you make your money?"

Matter-of-factly, Walker said, "Yes."

Now Michael understood. His mother was right, and he

was intrigued. A week or so later, when told he could earn as much as a thousand dollars a week by purloining navy secrets, he decided to do it. Walker was a domineering and demanding parent, and Michael craved his approval. He also craved easy money.

When he walked off the base with his first secret document hidden under his jacket, he was so scared that he almost vomited. But he got the document home to his father, who pronounced it "good." He stole another one the next week. "This is good," Walker said. "Keep up the flow. Things are looking good."

Walker and the KGB now had a new young spy.

John Walker's intuitive apprehensions about Jerry Whitworth were justified. In October 1983, without consulting or informing Walker, Whitworth retired from the navy. Several weeks later, he notified Walker by letter.

Whitworth still had film from his last cruise on the *Enterprise,* so Walker flew to California to pick it up before meeting the KGB in Vienna on February 4, 1984. His announcement that Whitworth unexpectedly had quit the navy stunned and mortified the KGB handler. Without minimizing the loss, Walker suggested that in time he could be coaxed back into the navy or a government job involving communications. He pointed out that Whitworth had received no money since September 1982 and recommended that the KGB pay him for the past fifteen months, which included his year on the *Enterprise.*

Meanwhile, all had not been lost. He expected great things from Michael and his new shipboard assignment on the *Nimitz.* Conceivably, Laura might be goaded back into the service. And maybe they could light a fire under Arthur.

As usual at the end of a meeting, the KGB gave him instructions for the next contact, this a drop near Washington, on April 15, 1984.

The KGB in the later years had raised Whitworth's payments to approximately four thousand dollars a month. Advised by Walker that he would be in touch with his contact in mid-April, Whitworth came to Norfolk expecting to receive at least sixty thousand dollars in back pay.

On Saturday night, April 15, Walker locked himself in a motel room and read a KGB message after unloading the drop. It reported that a goodly proportion of Whitworth's film from the *Enterprise* was worthless, unreadable. Whitworth was an excellent and experienced photographer. Over the years, he had photographed tens of thousands of documents. All of his film was very clear.

Now the KGB suspected, and upon reflection so did Walker, that Whitworth deliberately had fogged the film to extract extra payment. In explaining why the cash left in the drop was less than due, the KGB message said, "For D, zero."

The KGB also advised Walker that unless he signaled for an exchange earlier, their next contact would be in Vienna on January 19, 1985.

Driving nonstop, Walker arrived at his home in Norfolk just before noon. He took Whitworth into his den and told him about the faulty film. Then with scissors he cut out the part of the message pertaining to D, which Whitworth knew meant him, and let him read it. Whitworth turned ashen and trembled.

"Jerry, I'll try to change their minds," Walker said. "But it will be a while. I won't be talking to them until winter."

Back in California, Whitworth felt robbed and cheated. But what could he do? He decided he could write the FBI using an alias, and on May 7 he wrote the first RUS letter.

Michael boarded the *Nimitz,* based in Norfolk, in January 1984. During his first months, he worked in the engineering, then special services departments, where there was no classified information. Walker upbraided him, Michael later said, and made him "feel like shit" for not stealing any secrets. "You've already gone this far. Why not keep going?" Moreover, Michael was distressed because he had received no money for the documents he stole from the fighter squadron in 1983.

In April, after Whitworth left Norfolk, Walker telephoned Michael, who was living with his young bride, Rachel. "Come on over. I have your money."

On a desk Walker had several stacks of money, each totaling one thousand dollars, and Michael happily assumed all were for him. But Walker gave him only one stack. Recognizing Michael's disappointment and bitterness, Walker told him that if he desired more money, he had to produce. Then he showed him a document, which Michael thought came from a submarine. "Have you ever seen a Top Secret document before?" Michael understood the message. His father wanted Top Secret documents.

Finally, in August of 1984, Michael gained a transfer to the Operations Administrations Office and a little later also began to work in the nearby Strike Operations Office. In these operational offices were Top Secret and Secret documents galore. And Michael copied them freely. His main problem was finding a place to store them before he slipped them off the carrier to his father, who photographed them for the KGB.

As it turned out, Michael never received another payment after the one thousand dollars given him in April 1984. That thousand dollars would cost him twenty-five years of his life.

Shivering in another Vienna storm, Walker on the night of January 19, 1985, bluntly told his handler that he was through with street meetings. In response to earlier protests, his first handler told him that the KGB had no safe houses in Vienna and that they were safe on the street because always they were under the invisible protection of special surveillants. Now Walker declared that if the KGB could not find a haven in Vienna, it should sneak him across the Czech border, where they could talk at leisure and in comfort instead of "whispering in a goddamned blizzard."

Perhaps, shocked by the loss of Whitworth, someone in Moscow had rethought the whole case and concluded that Walker must be handled more delicately and Whitworth revived as a source.

Without hesitation, the Department 16 officer said, "Yes, next time we will go to Czechoslovakia."

Subsequently he stated — at least four times — "Tell Jerry he will be paid. Make him understand."

Money for Jerry as well as for Michael and John Walker would be delivered at a Maryland drop on May 19, 1985. The handler gave Walker the hand-printed instructions for the drop that would be his last.

The trial of Jerry Alfred Whitworth began in San Francisco on March 6, 1986. Two able and experienced lawyers, James Larson, whom Whitworth hired, and Tony Tamburello, appointed to assist at government expense, throughout fought tenaciously for their client. But had the trial been a prizefight, the referee would have stopped it early.

Prosecutors Buck Farmer and Leida Schoggen, assisted by John Dion and Lieutenant Alsup, marshaled more than two hundred witnesses and two thousand exhibits. The witnesses included experts on navy communications, cryptography, fleet operations, handwriting, documents, and the KGB; agents of the FBI, IRS, and Naval Intelligence; a distinguished professor of accounting and tax law; people who sold Whitworth expensive lingerie and hordes of Minox film; a representative of the Minox manufacturer from Germany. The prosecution witnesses also included Barbara, Laura, Michael, and John Walker, who proved to be a confident, unshakable witness.

Among the exhibits were the pay record, Walker's calendars, a classified document found in Walker's home with Whitworth's palm print on it. One of the most impressive was entitled "Analysis of Whitworth Involvement with John Anthony Walker 1975–1984." In it, Bill Smits, abetted by the magnificent research of Joe Wolfinger's team in Norfolk and Alex Seddio's IRS team in San Francisco, documented the basic outline of John Walker's story of the spy ring from 1975 on. The exhibits proving tax evasion were so overwhelming that the defense did not even contest the tax charges.

The morning of July 24, 1986, the jury foreman stood and announced, "We find the defendant guilty . . ."

Farmer banged his fist on the table, then turned and stared at Whitworth a few feet away as the foreman announced that the jury had found him guilty of seven counts of espionage and five counts of tax evasion.

As soon as the Federal Building opened on August 28, 1986, people congested the corridor outside the courtroom hoping to gain entrance for the sentencing. To Leida Schoggen fell the difficult assignment of deciding who among the hundreds of contributors to the prosecution would be allowed the few spaces reserved for the government. To the prosecution table she admitted, in addition to Farmer, Dion, Alsup, and herself, Bill Smits, John Peterson, and Bob Griego. Among those permitted on the one public bench allotted the government were Janet Fournier, Florence Poon, Shannon Hodges, Alex Seddio, and David Szady.

U.S. District Judge John P. Vukasin, Jr., a distinguished-looking white-haired jurist of Yugoslavian descent, spoke gravely. Since the trial ended, he said, he had thought every day about the sentencing of Whitworth, whom he termed "one of the most spectacular spies of the century." He summed up his thoughts thus: "Jerry Whitworth is a zero at his bones. He believes in nothing. His life is devoted to determining the wind direction and how he can make a profit from the coming storm . . . [he represents] the evil of banality."

Ordering Whitworth to stand, John Vukasin asked him if he wished to say anything. In a choked, barely audible voice Whitworth muttered, "Except to say I'm very, very sorry."

Thereupon the judge sentenced him to 365 years in prison and fined him $410,000. Whitworth first will be eligible for parole in 60 years, when he is 107 years old.

Whitworth, who worried about dying without anyone knowing how good a spy he was, at least could have the consolation that now people would know.

One great question remained: Would those in the U.S. government charged with assessing and repairing the damage the spies had caused recognize how good Whitworth and Walker were and do all necessary to remove the nation and the West from the mortal peril they created?

10

Picking Up
the Pieces

THE TASK OF ASSESSING the damage wrought by the
spies over a span of at least seventeen years was staggering enough to daunt the best minds and most in-
trepid spirits. The greatest difficulty arose from a natural impulse to disbelieve the unbelievable.

This impulse manifested itself in public and private statements made in Washington during the early summer of 1985.
Some of the pronouncements were remarkably similar to
those made in Germany and Japan during World War II.

Both the Germans and Japanese repeatedly received inti-
mations and explicit evidence that their ciphers were being
broken. Always, in the end, they dismissed the evidence and
took solace from a theoretical given: Their ciphers basically
were unbreakable. Thefts by the perfidious British Secret Service or isolated security lapses might cause temporary rup-
tures. But daily changes of keys, periodic modifications of
machines, revisions of the ciphers themselves, and mathematical odds precluded ongoing penetration of their enciphered communications. Or so they told themselves.

Historian Ronald Lewin observed that German leaders suffered from what sociologist Thorstein Veblen termed "trained incapacity." Professional instincts suggested that a catastrophe had befallen them. But as Lewin put it, "Their minds had been dragooned and regimented into the belief that Enigma was totally secure: Therefore, they were incapable of assessing objectively any indications that it had become insecure."

Similarly, despite unmistakable evidence that Walker and Whitworth *could* have given the Soviets all they needed to break American ciphers for more than a decade, Washington officialdom initially could not accept that the worst had happened. Admiral James D. Watkins, then chief of naval operations, in June articulated the prevailing navy judgment. The damage inflicted by the spy ring, he declared, was "very serious" but "not catastrophic."

However, on August 1, 1985, there occurred two events that would dramatically affect the ultimate American response to the Walker-Whitworth case. In Rome, Colonel Vitaly Yurchenko walked into the U.S. embassy. And in Washington, David Major became the first active FBI agent to serve on the National Security Council.

While teaching counterintelligence to other FBI agents, Major used to warn against bias that blinds one to facts or their import. "The struggle to disbelieve is eternal," he would say. "We struggle to disbelieve that which contradicts our predispositions."

Major learned early to face reality, to start where you are, however hard the beginning. His father, whom he revered, taught him by precept. The son of Hungarian immigrants, his father did not really master English until he was well into high school, and children sometimes ridiculed him as a "Hunkie" because of his thick accent. Nevertheless, he put himself through college and earned a degree in chemistry. He was proud of his education and his American citizenship, and he instilled the same pride into his son.

During the depression of the 1930s, Major's father lost his job and, like millions of other men, could not find another. "Don't worry," he told his family. "In America you always can find something to do." And he did. Touring upstate New York and western Pennsylvania as a song-and-dance man, he did quite well. When times grew better, he got a teaching job. By studying at night, he obtained a master's degree and at age forty-five a Ph.D. from Syracuse University.

Dave Major was a stocky kid with poor eyesight. Yet he flung himself into athletics, succeeding by raw energy and determination. He courted the prettiest girls, whom many other boys were afraid to approach, and attracted them by his intelligence, exuberant self-confidence, and ability to cope, whatever the circumstances.

The army granted him an ROTC scholarship with the provision that he could not serve with combat forces because of his inadequate vision. Having received his commission and a degree in biochemistry from Syracuse University in 1965, Major resolved to fight in Vietnam. He wangled his way out of the Chemical Corps into Armor and there, by dogged persistence, secured a waiver that allowed him to attend parachute school and join the Special Forces.

Jumped from second lieutenant to captain, Major took command of a company. His men knew him as a tough but fair commander who asked nothing of them he would not do himself.

Discharged in 1970, Major went to work as a chemist for the Du Pont company in Wilmington, Delaware. Du Pont was a good employer and life in Delaware pleasant. Yet in a few months Major concluded he never would be happy as a chemist. Being honest with himself, he acknowledged that there was only one thing he really wanted to do: fight for the United States the rest of his life.

On a Saturday morning, he talked to a CIA recruiter in

nearby Philadelphia. The recruiter said he probably could begin as a CIA trainee in early 1971. As a kind of afterthought he added, "You know, though, it seems to me that you're most interested in counterintelligence. In fairness to yourself, maybe you also ought to talk to the FBI."

After interrogating, testing, and investigating him, the FBI advised that he could join a class of new agents convening three weeks later. So Major chose the FBI. Of the fifty beginning agents in his class at Quantico, forty-eight had served as officers in Vietnam.

In the violent slums of Newark and on the brutal docks of Hoboken, New Jersey, Major learned to run agent operations against domestic and international terrorists, one of whom murdered a policeman in front of his house. Major also dueled with the New York residency of the KGB, whose operations often spilled over into New Jersey.

His performance there gained him a transfer to the Washington field office and the chance to learn on the streets from some of the best counterintelligence operatives in the FBI. He worked against all three principal components of the KGB in Washington: Line X, which steals scientific and technical secrets; Line KR, which endeavors to penetrate American intelligence; and Line PR, which strives to manipulate public policy and opinion. In the late 1970s he distinguished himself as one of the case officers successfully handling Arkady Shevchenko, who spied for the United States while undersecretary general of the United Nations.

The FBI in 1980 brought Major to headquarters to conduct counterintelligence seminars and advanced refresher courses, both in Washington and field offices. Waving his cigar like a baton and, upon making a point, thrusting it forward like a sword, he lectured throughout the country. In so doing, he came to know virtually everybody in FBI counterintelligence. By 1984, when the FBI put him in charge of counterintelligence in Baltimore, Major had formed professional and personal friendships with men who had decisive roles in the Walker-Whitworth case. Among them were John Martin, Bill Smits, David Szady, and Joe Wolfinger. They could and did speak frankly to each other, inside and outside regular channels.

Because John and Michael Walker were arraigned in Baltimore, the Baltimore field office had immediate jurisdiction over their cases. But most of the evidence the U.S. attorney's office in Baltimore required for prosecution still emanated from Norfolk, San Francisco, and Washington. So Major necessarily consulted continuously with Wolfinger, Szady, and Smits. He had no compunction about importuning them for information, day or night. Smits in turn had no compunction about impressing upon him the now unanimous judgment of the San Francisco team: It would be potentially suicidal folly to assume that Walker, Whitworth, and the Soviets had not done all they could have done, that the nation had not suffered a calamity which demanded radical remedial actions.

The shock produced by the arrests of the Walkers and Whitworth cemented a Reagan administration decision to place a top FBI counterintelligence expert on the National Security Council to advise it and the president. After interviewing three candidates nominated by the FBI, the NSC chose David Major.

He came to the White House with a complete understanding of the Walker-Whitworth case and without any predispositions to disbelieve the worst. On the contrary, his own review of all the available evidence, beginning with the RUS letters, convinced him that U.S. cipher systems had been widely compromised and still might be insecure.

In a briefing on August 7, 1985, Major so advised President Reagan. He also informed him that KGB defector Yurchenko had just reported that the Soviets had deciphered millions of secret American messages.

Shaking his head, the president asked, "How could this have happened?"

Major did not apologize for the FBI or the navy. He did point out a reality the Walker-Whitworth case starkly dramatized. The United States had permitted the Soviet Union and its satellite nations to station so many professional intelligence officers in the country that the FBI simply could not keep track of them all. To service Walker's drops, the KGB had sent a professional surveillant from the Seventh Directorate in Moscow, Aleksei Tkachenko. In Washington he did nothing untoward except venture out once or twice a year to the drop sites. His fellow KGB officers and the FBI alike put him down as a low-level administrator of no operational importance. The FBI ignored him because common sense dictated that it concentrate its limited resources on officers known to be important operatives. So long as the imbalance of strength between the FBI and Soviet bloc services persisted in the United States, there could be no guarantee against recurrence of a Walker-type case.

From this and subsequent briefings Major delivered to the president, important decisions flowed. The word went out from the National Security Council that Ronald Reagan wanted the truth about the Walker-Whitworth case, whatever the consequences, that he was interested in salvaging the future rather than bemoaning the past. The president resolved to abolish the "divine right" claimed by the Soviets to keep legions of spies in the United States and spy upon America from within. When Secretary of Defense Caspar Weinberger made the politically unpopular decision to negotiate for the cooperation of John Walker, he did so with the support of the National Security Council and the president.

Today, pursuant to presidential instructions, learned men

and women at the Pentagon and NSA assay the wreckage, trying to ascertain the consequences of all that has been lost. Among those laboring to pick up the pieces and repair shattered defenses, two men bear some of the gravest responsibilities. They are Rear Admiral William O. Studeman and Richard Haver, director and deputy director of the Office of Naval Intelligence.

After the American Civil War and the Franco-Prussian War, many Germans immigrated to the United States, and some established colonies in Texas. Admiral Chester Nimitz came from this stock and so did Bill Studeman's father. The elder Studeman was a pioneer aviator, flying in World War I, then helping build Pan American into what once was the world's premier international airline. And he imbued his son with his own ethos, which exalted work, honesty, "duty, honor, country."

Commissioned an ensign in 1963, Studeman rose spectacularly, becoming in 1983 one of the youngest admirals in navy history. Along the way, his blunt candor and rigid insistence upon purity sometimes bruised feelings. Once he spotted on the desk of a subordinate a coffee cup stamped with the imprimatur of a defense contractor. He rebuked the officer for accepting the cup as a present. "We don't take anything from anybody; not a nickel."

Self-effacing, Admiral Studeman shunned personal publicity and often credited subordinates with his successes. He declined this author's request for an interview, citing in writing four reasons. "Most importantly, the Navy is a proud service. The glorification of naval personnel in this case would be inconsistent with the fact that the Walker-Whitworth spy ring, one of the most damaging and revulsive in U.S. history, was able to function, endure and flourish so long and successfully in the environment of the naval service."

In other words, in Studeman's view, the shame with which

the Walkers and Whitworth stained the navy allows no acclaim for anyone in the navy, no matter how commendable their actions.

The nation, however, needs to know about some actions.

When Admiral Studeman took over Naval Intelligence in September 1985, the Walker-Whitworth case eclipsed all problems before him. He issued orders that echoed those of the president: We must find out the truth, however horrendous it may be.

With Studeman's support, Secretary of Defense Weinberger designated Haver as the chief damage assessment officer. Growing up in the New Jersey suburbs of New York City, Richard Haver dreamed of being a naval officer. The U.S. Naval Academy turned him down because of his imperfect eyesight. So he attended Johns Hopkins University, where he studied history and played basketball, baseball, and lacrosse. Upon graduation in 1968, he again tried the navy, and with a war on it this time accepted him.

As an electronics intelligence officer, Haver flew missions over Vietnam for almost two years. In Washington in 1972, Admiral Bobby R. Inman, who was to become director of the NSA and later deputy director of the CIA, took an interest in Haver, as he had in young Studeman. He dissuaded him from his plan to enter law school and convinced him instead to join Naval Intelligence as a civilian.

Haver's meteoric rise paralleled that of Studeman, and in 1984 he became the first civilian ever to be appointed deputy director of Naval Intelligence. During his intelligence career, he spent protracted periods at the NSA and thus well understood the world of ciphers.

Beginning in the early 1970s, Haver periodically saw signs that "something was wrong," that the Soviets knew things they should not have known. Privately, he sometimes wondered about the security of U.S. communications. But like

Smits and Peterson in 1984, he had no proof. Discovery of the Walker-Whitworth espionage suddenly made everything clear. Says Haver, "It was like opening the sluice gates of understanding of the past."

Once Studeman and Haver were fully in charge, statements about the Walker-Whitworth case issuing from the Pentagon changed radically. They frankly acknowledged that the espionage constituted an unmitigated disaster of measureless dimensions.

The continuing damage assessment is being conducted in the strictest secrecy, and many conclusions probably will be kept secret. But public statements by responsible authorities, including Studeman, suggest some possibilities and probabilities.

Analysts surveying the havoc with unbiased eyes have affirmed the validity of what Lieutenant Alsup told John Martin in San Francisco. For the revelations of Yurchenko coupled with those of John Walker smashed any illusions that the Soviets had not been reading secret American ciphers since 1968. One conversation in Vienna between Walker and his KGB case officer said it all, the one in which the KGB officer stated that although the Soviets suddenly could not break the KWR-37 system, "with the other systems, there is no problem."

Further, analysts concluded that Walker and Whitworth had endowed the Soviets with such insights into the concepts as well as the practical workings of American cipher systems that they probably were able to break some *without* the key. This meant that even though the Soviets no longer were receiving key material, they still might be able to read messages transmitted through the compromised systems.

Both Secretary of the Navy John Lehman and Admiral Studeman have stated that communications compromises caused by Walker may have cost American lives in Vietnam.

Studeman states they could have been "responsible for ineffective air strikes, downed aircraft, abandoned targets, and infantry losses."

However, it would seem doubtful that the Walker-Whitworth espionage decisively influenced the outcome of the Vietnam War. South Vietnam fell in April 1975 in consequence of a political decision to withdraw all American combat forces in 1973. While the conquest of South Vietnam and Cambodia represented a ruinous defeat of American geopolitical policy, it did not represent a defeat of American arms, contrary to what those who craved communist victory now are fond of saying.

There is no doubt that the unveiling of virtually all navy secrets contributed significantly to the development of the modern Soviet navy and the diminution of the U.S. technological lead in important spheres. After the humiliation of the Cuban missile crisis in 1962, the Soviet Union determined to build an oceangoing fleet capable of projecting Soviet power throughout the world and challenging the U.S. Navy on all seas. Heretofore, the Soviet navy had been a comparatively small and primitive force oriented toward coastal defense. The Soviets did not have the historic experience and accumulated expertise of the seafaring Western nations, which long had maintained large, far-ranging battle fleets. The skill and rapidity with which the Soviets built a blue-water navy, the quality of their ships and submarines, and the sophistication of their tactics surprised Western observers. Their success is now less mystifying. The first ships of the new Soviet navy began coming into service about the time John Walker began the hemorrhage of navy secrets. Thereafter, the Soviets were able to study and learn at their convenience from the world's best teacher: the U.S. Navy.

Conceivably, John Walker and Jerry Whitworth influenced Soviet internal affairs. Yuri Andropov became chairman of the KGB in May 1967 and, before departing in 1982 to become ruler of the Soviet Union, served longer than any other boss of the state security apparatus. Yurchenko characterized the Walker case, which appears to have begun shortly after Andropov took control of the KGB, as the greatest in the history of the KGB. Certainly, the case enhanced his standing, and it may have abetted his ascension to power.

Yurchenko reported that he authoritatively was told that in the event of war, the intelligence Walker and Whitworth imparted would have had "devastating consequences for the United States." Everybody agrees.

"Had we been engaged in any conflict with the Soviets, it could have had the devastating consequences that Ultra had for the Germans," declares Secretary Lehman. (Ultra was the British code term for all intelligence emanating from broken German ciphers in World War II.)

Admiral Studeman asserts that the thefts by Walker and Whitworth created "powerful war-winning implications for the Soviet side."

Perhaps the future is of more concern than the past. At immense cost, machines, keys, frequencies, and methods have been modified. But the Soviets over seventeen years amassed such comprehensive knowledge of American communications, cipher machines, and systems that doubts arise about the security of any except totally new systems.

In an affidavit submitted to the federal court in San Francisco, Studeman stated that Whitworth "jeopardized the backbone of this country's national defense." He added: "Recovery from the Walker-Whitworth espionage will take years and millions of taxpayer dollars. Even given these expenditures, we will likely never know the true extent to which our capabilities have been impaired by the traitorous and infamous acts of Jerry Whitworth."

To find a final prosecution witness who could most authoritatively and clearly explain to the jury the damage inflicted by the spy ring, Buck Farmer searched the American military and intelligence communities. He finally selected George A. Carver, a former deputy to the director of Central Intelligence. A scholarly man with a doctoral degree from Oxford University, Carver spent much of his twenty-four-year career as an intelligence officer in cryptography and communications.

Carver emphasized that the Soviets can continue to exploit the data supplied by Walker and Whitworth "for years and even decades." He summarized the damage thus: "The United States will have to invest an enormous amount of time and resources changing systems, changing procedures, at great dislocation. It can never be positive that it has locked all the barn doors to keep future horses from straying. I cannot be totally confident about the security of its communications, particularly its military and especially its naval communications. And the damage thus done, in my opinion, could significantly, if not irrevocably, tilt the very strategic balance on which our survival as a nation depends."

While relaying such portentous assessments of the Walker-Whitworth case to President Reagan, Major also had to report to him other costly losses caused by Edward Lee Howard and Ronald Pelton, the former CIA and NSA employees turned spies. Additionally, the FBI in the fall of 1985 began pursuing still other ominous leads supplied by Yurchenko, and European allies shared disturbing new intelligence about Soviet espionage worldwide.

But it was the Walker-Whitworth case that had the greatest psychological impact in the White House and Congress. Usually, an espionage case generates a brief flurry of headlines, then quickly sinks from public sight and consciousness. But the Walker-Whitworth case would not go away. In it, all but

213

the most obtuse or disingenuous could see ruinous damage to the country. Here was proof that espionage is not merely an inconsequential game played by inveterate cold warriors who refuse to grow up but a deadly business that can affect the survival of the nation. The Walker-Whitworth case, together with all the others, created for the first time in many years genuine bipartisan support for effective countermeasures against the KGB.

The Reagan administration decided to start by cutting down the legion of KGB and GRU officers enjoying diplomatic immunity in the United States. In March 1986, the same month Whitworth's trial opened in San Francisco, it informed the Soviets that they would have to remove 105 "diplomats" from their bloated mission to the United Nations in New York. However, both the tone of the announcement and the terms of the mandated reduction were conciliatory. To spare the Soviets sudden disruption, the United States would allow them to withdraw their "diplomats" gradually: 25 by October 1, 1986; an additional 25 by April 1, 1987; another 25 by October 1, 1987; and the final 30 by April 1, 1988.

On September 12, 1986, with the deadline for the first departures nearing, the Soviet ambassador to the United Nations, Aleksandr M. Belonogov, declared that the reduction was "absolutely illegal" and that the Soviets were "not making any preparations" to comply with it. In the words of David Major, the Soviets thereby "stepped on their dong."

President Reagan seethed. The Soviets were presuming to tell the United States government what it could do in its own country. They in effect were thumbing their nose at the president and saying, "We will keep as many of our people in New York as we please."

In the Oval Office, the president said to advisers, "I want to bloody the KGB."

214

Eyes brightening, cigar waving, Major leaned forward and said, "How about decapitation?"

The FBI promptly gave the NSC a list of the 25 men who constituted the brains and sinews of the Soviet espionage apparatus in New York. Included were the KGB and GRU residents and their deputies; the KGB chiefs of Line PR, Line X, and Line KR; and the security officer, cipher clerks, and signal officers overseeing a massive electronic eavesdropping operation. The United States then formally expelled all 25, ordering them out of the country by October 1.* The Soviets were aghast that the FBI knew exactly who was who in their residencies and more aghast at the mass expulsion, unprecedented in the history of U.S.–Soviet relations. However, while railing and issuing vague threats, they had no choice except to comply.

Privately, Secretary of State George P. Shultz cautioned the Soviets not to retaliate lest they bring down on themselves the further wrath of Ronald Reagan. "The president's powder is dry," he said. Nevertheless, the Soviets on Sunday, October 19, did retaliate by ousting from Moscow five American diplomats, none of whom, incidentally, was an intelligence officer. (Says an NSC staff member, "They purposely did it on Sunday just to screw up our weekend.")

At 9:30 A.M. the next day, Secretary Shultz, Attorney General Edwin Meese, CIA Director William Casey, and National Security Adviser John Poindexter gathered with the president in the Oval Office. There was unanimous agreement. The Soviets had confronted the United States with both an opportunity and a necessity. They must be shown that U.S. tolerance

*Anyone formally expelled or declared persona non grata may not return to the United States. Because of agreements among Western allies, neither may the individual serve in any other Western country.

of rampant espionage, of their presumed right to keep hundreds of KGB officers in America, had ended.

The maximum number of U.S. diplomats allowed in Moscow and Leningrad was 251. In addition to some 300 "diplomats" at their United Nations mission and an equal number of Soviet nationals employed by the UN Secretariat in New York, the Soviets had 325 diplomats accredited in Washington and San Francisco. The president and his council decided, in one fell swoop, to slash the number of Soviet diplomats in Washington and San Francisco to 251.

A reduction of 19 could be effected simply by not allowing 19 who were home on leave to return. That meant 55 needed to be expelled.

Again the FBI was ready with a list of key names. The 55 persons listed comprised the KGB and GRU leadership in Washington and the entire KGB residency in San Francisco. On Tuesday, October 21, the United States announced the expulsion of all 55.

The decapitation of the KGB in the United States was complete; the organization was totally leaderless and, because of the ouster of most cipher clerks, barely able to communicate by radio with Moscow. Moreover, Secretary Shultz informed the Soviets that they would not be permitted to replace the KGB and GRU leaders. The Soviets attempted to send new KGB and GRU residents to New York, but the two were denied entry.

As of October 21, the United States had dictated an overall reduction of 179 KGB and GRU officers: 74 from Washington and San Francisco (55 expelled; 19 not allowed to return); 25 from the UN mission; plus 80 more who would have to leave the UN mission in stages by April 1, 1988. If the Soviets again retaliated by kicking out additional Americans, the administration intended to eliminate even more Soviet intelligence personnel. Making ready, the FBI submitted a third list, consisting of the best of the remaining operatives.

However, the Soviets instead did something for which the Reagan administration could not have hoped. A secret investigation of the U.S. embassy in Moscow had disclosed appalling security conditions. The embassy was infested with hidden microphones. The KGB had implanted in embassy typewriters devices that enabled it to read everything printed on them. And Soviet employees, almost all of them KGB officers or coopted agents, daily roamed the embassy.

An investigator brought back a photograph of one of them. Her name was Raya. She was a beautiful, seductive blonde. Handing her picture to President Reagan, the investigator said, "Raya is a KGB colonel."

"She has got to go," the president said.

However, the State Department, whose Foreign Service personnel coveted the convenience of Soviet employees and servants, fiercely resisted efforts by the president and Congress to remove the embassy workers. Dragging its feet in hope that a post-Reagan administration would not be so heartless, the State Department had reluctantly acquiesced to some gradual reductions but certainly not dismissal of all Soviet employees.

On October 23, though, Soviet ruler Mikhail Gorbachev, to spite the Americans for the latest expulsions, withdrew all 260 Soviet workers employed by the United States in Moscow and Leningrad. Henceforth, the poor diplomats would have to drive their own cars, cook their own cheeseburgers, and do their own translating without any help from the KGB. Gorbachev had done for the United States what the president and Congress had been unable to do!

The events of the autumn of 1986 were important in that they dramatically diminished the capability of the Soviet

Union to direct espionage operations from within the United States. They were even more important for what they signified — a historic change in American policy toward Soviet espionage.

Still, in the eyes of all who truly understand what John Walker and Jerry Whitworth did, the specter of their treason remains. It will remain and haunt them until the U.S. government can completely assure itself and the nation that the sanctity of American communications has been restored. Until that is done, no one can be sure that what happened to the Germans and Japanese in World War II may not someday happen to the West.

Epilogue

Those knowledgeable about the subject say that in prison, life is hardest for child molesters, spies, "snitches," defrocked cops, and weak young men.

Michael Walker, a short, frail youth, entered prison at age twenty-three. He still looks so childlike and is so adept at projecting an image of misguided innocence, that a court reporter wept as she transcribed his testimony in the Whitworth trial. Predatory criminals caged for life may regard him differently.

In formalizing Michael's sentence of twenty-five years' imprisonment, Judge Alexander Harvey 2d regarded him with cold contempt. Never, he declared, should Michael be paroled. Reading an affidavit submitted by Rear Admiral Studeman, Judge Harvey perhaps thought of other young people Michael had betrayed and his greed for profits from the betrayal.

The affidavit disclosed, for the first time, that Michael Walker stole more than fifteen hundred secret documents. The documents revealed how and when the navy would use nuclear weapons; characteristics of the defensive and offensive weapons systems on U.S. ships; targets the navy would assault in wartime; just how ships avoid detection by the Soviets; precisely how the United States planned to react to specific emergencies; previously hidden vulnerabilities of the United States and the Soviet Union; secrets that would enable the Soviets to achieve surprise and tactical advantage in combat.

"We may never know the full extent of the damage done by Michael Walker's breach of trust," Admiral Studeman concluded. "From what we do know, it is certain that he was willing to jeopardize the lives of his shipmates and the very ability of our country to defend itself."

Michael told the FBI that for a while he was unproductive as a spy. He explained that he was "having so much fun" with his new wife. For the next twenty-five years, he will not enjoy the company of his wife or any other woman.

For Arthur Walker, life in prison already has proven to be hard. Inmates at Lewisburg, Pennsylvania, repeatedly threatened to kill "the traitor." So in the fall of 1986, authorities transferred him to the federal penitentiary in Terre Haute, Indiana.

Absent a deal with the Soviet Union, parole boards do not let spies out early. Sentenced in August 1985 to three life terms, Arthur doubtless will die in prison, naturally or violently. He very well may die without ever having told the truth.

Arthur repeatedly has claimed that he did not engage in espionage while in the navy or prior to 1980, that before then he knew nothing about John Walker's spying. As late as November 1986, he swore to this story in an affidavit. But several facts challenge him.

Barbara and Laura Walker consistently have told investigators the truth insofar as they can remember it. None of their substantive statements has been found in error. Barbara reported that during a conversation with Arthur in 1969 she bewailed her husband's spying. She explicitly recalled that

Arthur in 1969 remarked, "If it's any consolation to you, I did the same thing, only on a smaller scale and for a shorter period of time."

Once when she upbraided John Walker for spying, he commented, "You'd be surprised who got me started."

Laura remembers her father telling her that Arthur persuaded him to reenlist in the navy back in 1968 when the family was experiencing severe financial problems. She also remembers that the money problems vanished soon after he reenlisted. During 1968 and 1969, according to Laura, Arthur and his family frequently visited her family. During the visits Arthur and her father always sequestered themselves and talked privately. Wives and children of both understood they were not to be interrupted.

Polygraph examinations indicate that Arthur consistently has lied when asked if he spied while in the navy.

John Walker's basic account of his espionage subsequent to 1968 has been so thoroughly and independently corroborated that investigators do not doubt its essence. Vitaly Yurchenko, whose information proved accurate in so many other important areas, confirmed that records in Moscow showed that Walker did visit the Soviet embassy in Washington.

However, polygraph tests in the fall of 1986 indicated that Walker was deceptive in his answers to questions about espionage before 1968, meetings with hostile intelligence officers between 1968 and 1976, and possibly about involvement with still other spies. So there may be somewhat more to the history of the Walker spy ring than is known. But what is unknown concerns a time almost twenty years past. And the unknown could not possibly be any worse than the known.

One morning when John Walker was being led from a Howard County jail for interrogation in Baltimore, prisoners started shouting, "There's the traitor! Kill him! Kill him!"

Marked as both a traitor and a snitch, Walker is likely to hear such taunts and threats in prison at Lewisburg, Pennsylvania, and for the rest of his life.

For a while before his testimony in the Whitworth trial, Walker was lodged in the high-rise Metropolitan Correctional Center in San Diego. From outside, it looks like an expensive apartment building, and it is about as modern and humane as a prison can be. Walker boasted about the quality of the food and exercise facilities. Then he dropped all pretenses and to FBI agents said, "Let's face it. Prison is hell." Unless he escapes, there is no chance John Walker ever again will experience life outside prison.

Jerry Whitworth, during interrogations after his sentencing, wept and accused FBI agents of being "self-righteous." En route to Leavenworth prison in Kansas, he wrote Bill Smits from Reno, Oklahoma, sanctimoniously trying to exonerate himself.

Because Judge Vukasin did not request a presentencing report on Whitworth, a prison counselor at Leavenworth telephoned Farmer for background information. "I'm worried about Mr. Whitworth's prison career," he said. "Mr. Farmer, this is a punitive prison. It's a bad place." It is the place where Jerry Whitworth for the rest of his life can reflect upon "how good" he was.

The men and women who gave so much of themselves to breaking the ring have returned to their normal lives.

Barbara Walker quit drinking and is discovering the joys of freedom from addiction. Always, though, she lives with the pain of knowing that had she spoken to the FBI before 1983, her son would not now be in prison, his life largely over.

Laura Walker recovered her son from her estranged husband and now works for the Christian Broadcasting Network in Norfolk. She harbors no hatred for her father; neither, though, does she regret having helped to imprison him. "I wish for him the same that I wish for every other human being: God's forgiveness and salvation. Better to spend a lifetime in prison than eternity in Hell."

Janet and Pierre Fournier vacationed recently in Paris. French counterintelligence officers overwhelmed them with hospitality, taking them into their homes and delightful cafés seldom seen by tourists. Janet Fournier, who started it all, came back from her second honeymoon radiant and happy.

Alex Seddio, the IRS "Tasmanian Devil," and his stunningly beautiful wife, who is of Chinese descent, looked forward to the birth of their second child.

The navy nominated Lieutenant Alsup for a medal and assigned him to duty with the National Security Agency at Fort Meade, Maryland. He and Mary Jane bought a new house in nearby Columbia. Now colleagues listen to Alsup talk endlessly about both his first baby and the second child expected in June 1987.

The FBI put David Szady in charge of its office in Palo Alto, California. His son in the fall of 1986 enrolled at Princeton, starred on the freshman football team, and excelled in senior math courses.

The Justice Department did honor John Martin as the most outstanding employee of 1985. He later took his appealing blond wife, Carol, and two teenage sons on a fishing trip. He also took along Stanislav Levchenko, who has inspired the older boy to begin Russian studies.

To the great loss of the FBI and the nation, Bill Smits announced that upon reaching the age of fifty in January 1987, he would retire. A lucrative career awaits him in private industry, which he will advise about dealing with the Soviet bloc and protecting corporate secrets. No longer will he fly in the back of the airplane.

The FBI reassigned Beverly Andress to counterintelligence in Washington, where she can live with her husband.

Joe Wolfinger remains contentedly in Norfolk, enjoying his work and family. He remarked after Walker was led from court to prison, "You know, his children always called him Jaws. Mine call me Daddy."

Buck Farmer and Leida flew to the French Alps, then took the fast train to Paris. On a starlit night in a little café on the Left Bank, Buck asked, "Would you marry me?"

"Don't be silly, Buck. Of course, I would marry you. I love you."

"I'm serious, will you marry me?"

"Sure."

Fumbling in his jacket pocket, Buck failed to find what he was looking for. He excused himself and found it in his raincoat. Returning, he slipped an engagement ring on Leida's finger.

Notes

The notes identify the bases for principal statements of fact and narrative passages in the book.

In the notes, *Transcript* refers to the fifty-five-volume transcript of the trial of Jerry Whitworth conducted in U.S. District Court, San Francisco, from March 24 to July 24, 1986 (*United States of America* v. *Jerry Alfred Whitworth,* No. CR-85-552 JVP).

Exhibit, followed by a designation, refers to a specific exhibit introduced as evidence during the trial.

FBI Interview, followed by a date, refers to a declassified summary of an FBI interview made available to prosecution and defense attorneys.

Interview refers to an interview conducted by the author. Unless otherwise specified, conversations quoted derive from recollections of one or more of the named participants as reported to the author.

Chapter 1: A Letter From RUS

The actions, conversations, and background of Janet Fournier, John Peterson, and William Smits are derived from interviews with Fournier, Peterson, and Smits, as well as with superiors and colleagues of all three.

page
3 FBI ignored Oswald letter: Communication from FBI director to attorney general, dated July 29, 1975.

4–21 RUS letters: The RUS letters and FBI responses are reproduced in Exhibits A-400-A through A-400-I.

16 Statements by former Soviet colonel: Interview with Assistant U.S. Attorney William S. Farmer, San Francisco.

16–17 Department 16: Interviews with Stanislav Levchenko and Smits; also see John Barron, *The KGB Today* (New York: Reader's Digest Press, 1983).

19–20 Miron analysis: Declassified copy of analysis.

Chapter 2: Something Is Wrong

page

23 Major's conversation with admiral: Interview with David Major.

24 New Soviet submarines: Interview with Richard Haver, deputy director, Office of Naval Intelligence; *Soviet Military Power,* analysis issued by Department of Defense, September 1981.
Soviets awaiting sorties by U.S. submarines: Interview with Haver.
Bishop allegations: *Daily Gleaner* (St. George's, Grenada), May 12, 1979.

24–25 Aborted U.S. raid on Iran: Multiple intelligence sources.

30–31 Lord quotation: Walter Lord, *Incredible Victory* (New York: Harper & Row, 1967), ix–x.

31 U.S. entry into Japanese naval cipher: Ronald Lewin, *The American Magic* (New York: Farrar, Straus & Giroux, 1982).
Lewin quotation: *American Magic,* 96.

31–33 Battle of Midway: Edwin T. Layton, *And I Was There* (New York: William Morrow, 1985); Lewin, *American Magic*; Lord, *Incredible Victory*; Gordon W. Prange, *Miracle at Midway* (New York: McGraw-Hill, 1982).

33 Destruction of Japanese merchant fleet: Lewin, *American Magic,* 213–225.

34 Origins of Enigma: F. W. Winterbotham, *The Ultra Secret* (New York: Harper & Row, 1974), 10–11.
Ultra contributions to Battle of Britain: Ronald Lewin, *Ultra Goes to War* (London: Book Club Associates, 1978), 73–91.

34–35 Capture of data from *U-110*: Lewin, *American Magic,* 23.

35–36 Ultra contributions to Battle of Atlantic: Lewin, *Ultra Goes to War,* 208–220.

36 British control of German agents: Lewin, *Ultra Goes to War,* 301–321; J. C. Masterman, *The Double-Cross System in the War of 1939 to 1945* (New Haven and London: Yale University Press, 1972), 156–163.

38 Battle of Avranches Gap: Omar N. Bradley, *A Soldier's Story* (New York: Henry Holt, 1951), 370–372, 383; Winterbotham, *Ultra Secret,* 146–158.

39 Smits apprehensions: Interview with Smits.

Chapter 3: A Terrible Secret

page

40ff. Barbara Walker background and travails: FBI Interviews of Barbara Walker, March 19, 1985, and April 4–5, 1985; Transcript, Barbara Walker testimony, pp. 33–3624–25, 33–3638–39, 33–3649, 33–3654–55.

41–42 Laura Walker background: FBI Interviews of Laura Walker March 7–8, 1985; transcripts of CBN "700 Club" programs June 18–19, 1985; Transcript, p. 36–3931.

43 Barbara Walker account of John Walker at drops: Transcript, pp. 33–3642–45; FBI Interview, March 19, 1985.

43–44 FBI reaction to Barbara Walker's first revelations: Transcript, pp. 17–2097–98; interviews with David Szady, David Major, Joseph Wolfinger, John Martin, John Dion.

45–46 Joseph Wolfinger background: Interview with Szady; confirmed by Wolfinger.

47ff. David Szady background: Interviews with Wolfinger, Major, A. Jackson Lowe, and Szady.

52–53 Laura Walker statements to FBI: FBI Interview, March 7, 1985.
John Walker overtures to Laura Walker: FBI Interview, March 7, 1985; Transcript, pp. 35–3903, 33–3906–08.

54–56 Barbara Walker statements to FBI: FBI Interview, March 19, 1985; Transcript, p. 33–3645.

56 Laura Walker telephone conversation with John Walker: Declassified FBI report of investigation, March 25, 1985, by Paul W. Culligan, Charles B. Wagner, and Robert W. Hunter.

58 Szady approach to judge: Interview with Szady.

58–59 Characterization of agents Robert Hunter and Beverly Andress: Interviews with Wolfinger and Szady.

59–60 Conversation between Barbara and John Walker in Norfolk: FBI Interviews, April 8, 10, 12, 1985.

61 Barbara Walker resolve to enter hospital: FBI Interviews, April 4–5, 1985.

61–62 John Walker naval record: Affidavit of Rear Admiral William O. Studeman, director of Naval Intelligence, November 4, 1986, submitted to U.S. District Court, Baltimore; declassified U.S. Navy interview of John Walker dated December 12, 1985; Transcript, pp. 12–1462–69, 12–1481–85, 29–3216.

63 John Walker burglaries: Lackawanna (Pa.) County Juvenile Court records.

John Walker attempt to prostitute wife: FBI Interview, Laura Walker, April 4, 1985.

64 John Walker letter: Excerpts from taped message from Walker to son, Michael.

Chapter 4: Unmasking RUS

page

66ff. Conversations between Smits and Peterson: Interviews with both.

66–67 Harper case: FBI press release, October 17, 1983; Senate Permanent Subcommittee on Investigation hearings, December 3, 1985; interview with Smits.

69 FBI advertisements: Exhibit A-400-I.

FBI summaries and references to "Wentworth": FBI Interviews, April 4, 5, 8, 1985; Mary 10, 1985.

70 Robert Griego background: Interviews with Griego, Leida Schoggen, Peterson, and Smits.

71–75 passim Griego investigations: Interviews with Griego and Smits.

71 FBI Analytical Unit conclusions: Interviews with Szady, Smits, and Peterson.

73–74 Laura Walker statements to FBI: FBI Interview, May 10, 1985.

75 Whitworth naval record: Untitled summary prepared by U.S. Navy for FBI and Department of Justice.

Chapter 5: "It's Incredible"

page

80 John Walker statements: The author has had no access to tapes of intercepted telephone conversations. Each of the statements quoted was made in the presence of assistant U.S. attorneys Farmer and Schoggen or FBI agents Peterson and Griego and reported to the author by them; Wolfinger confirms that the quoted statements are typical of those heard in the intercepts.

81 Walker reaction to death of aunt: Interviews with Wolfinger and Szady.

82ff. Wolfinger actions during surveillance: Interview with Wolfinger.

83 FBI contingency plan: Interviews with Lowe, Szady, and Wolfinger.

83ff. Szady actions: Transcript, pp. 17–2062–63; interview with Szady.

85ff. Details of surveillance in Maryland: Transcript, pp. 17–2060–2114; interviews with Szady, Lowe, and Wolfinger.

87–88 Identification and actions of Aleksei Tkachenko: Transcript, pp. 17–2071–77.

89 John Dion background: Interviews with Dion and Martin.

90 Examination of documents at FBI headquarters: Transcript, pp. 23–2701–03; interviews with Dion and Jerry Richards.

90–92 John Walker letter to KGB: Exhibit A-1-A; Transcript, pp. 26–3104, 26–3106–07.

93–95 Arrest of Walker: Transcript, pp. 17–2083, 17–2123–45; interviews with Lowe and Szady.

Chapter 6: Unraveling the Net

page

98–101 John Martin background: Justice Department biography of Martin; statements of Attorney General Edwin Meese upon occasion of Martin's being honored as most outstanding employee of Justice Department; interviews with Joel Lisker, general counsel, Senate Subcommittee on Security and Terrorism, John Dion, Carol Martin, and Martin.

98 Civil rights investigation: Don Whitehead, *Attack on Terror* (New York: Funk & Wagnalls, 1970), 37, 38, 260, 280, 282.

99–100 Arrest of KGB officers: *United States* v. *Enger,* 473 F. Supp. (D. N.J. 1978).

100–101 Billy Carter acceptance of money from Libya: 1979 *New York Times Index,* 231–232, 237.

101–105 Peterson-McElwee interview of Whitworth: Transcript, pp. 18–2269–76, 18–2283; declassified FBI report of interview dictated May 22, 1985, by John P. Peterson and Michael S. McElwee.

105–106 Search of Walker's house: Transcript, pp. 20–2473, 20–2052; interview with Jerry Richards.

106 Walker notations of code for sources: Exhibit A-1-B.

108–109 Arthur Walker statements: Transcript, pp. 35–3821–28, 35–3882.

110–111 Interrogation of Michael Walker: Transcript, pp. 37–4042, 37–4085–86; interview with Russell Nelson, special agent, Naval Investigative Service.

111 Conversation between Michael and Rachel Walker: Interview with David Major.

Chapter 7: Reconstructing a Disaster

page

113 Arthur Walker admits supplying classified documents: Transcript, pp. 35–3821, 35–3833.
Whitworth access: RUS letter dated May 7, 1984; untitled U.S. Navy summary of Whitworth naval record.

114 Designation of Whitworth as "D": Transcript, p. 31–3486.

115ff. Background of William Farmer: Interviews with Mr. and Mrs. William S. Farmer, Sr., Schoggen, Farmer, Martin, and Dion.

119–120 Background and characterization of Leida Schoggen: Interviews with Farmer, Griego, Martin, Dion, and Schoggen.

121 Arrest of Whitworth: Interviews with Farmer and Dion; *Los Angeles Times,* June 5, 1985.

121–122 Letter to Whitworth: Copy provided by Schoggen; reprinted with permission of writer.

122–128 Whitworth background: Interviews with Farmer, Schoggen, Peterson, and Lieutenant James Alsup. An excellent article about Whitworth's early life written by Doug Struck appeared in the *Baltimore Sun*, June 12, 1985.

124 Statements by Master Chief Bennett: Transcript, pp. 12–1404, 12–1456–57.

125 Whitworth investments: Transcript, pp. 41–4640–43, 41–4659–65.

126 Whitworth letter to Senator Byrd: Copy provided by Farmer.

127–128 Whitworth naval assignments and duties: Untitled U.S. Navy summary.

128–129 James Alsup background: Interviews with Alsup and Farmer.

129–132 Data recovered from Walker's house: Transcript, pp. 18–2226, 18–2233–38, 18–2198.

130 Recognition of pay records: Exhibits A-22-E, A-22-HI; interviews with Dion, Smits, Peterson, Griego, Farmer, and Schoggen; Transcript, pp. 18–2186–87.

132–133 Formation of IRS team: Interviews with Farmer Alex Seddio, Barron Fong, Floyd Hobbs, and Florence Poon.

133–134 Cable to Whitworth: Copy provided by Farmer.

134 Rental of Rolls-Royce: Transcript, pp. 41–4610–11. Purchase of lingerie: Transcript, pp. 38–4232–34.

Chapter 8: Revelations from Moscow

page

138–139 Vitaly Yurchenko at Danker's: Interview with Martin; other FBI sources.

139 Status of security officer in Soviet embassy: Interviews with Levchenko and Alex Costa.

140–141 Yurchenko duties at KGB headquarters 1980–85: Central Intelligence Agency public statement, December 1985.

142 Rescue of Gorzdievski: The British Broadcasting Corporation on November 11, 1985, reported that British intelligence had spirited Gorzdievski out of Moscow (*Washington Times*, No-

vember 12, 1985). European and U.S. intelligence sources have confirmed to the author that Yurchenko provided critical information prompting the British action, and that Yurchenko for some time had been a British agent. Research has failed to confirm that Gorzdievski was a British agent as early as the 1970s.

143–145 Howard case: The most comprehensive report to date was written by David Wise, *New York Times Magazine*, November 2, 1986. Heretofore unpublished accounts of Howard's meeting with the KGB in Vienna on August 3, 1985, and the exact nature of the lapse in FBI surveillance emanate from confidential U.S. intelligence sources.

146–147 Pelton case: Author's account is based on information from U.S. intelligence sources, which generally comports with chronology published by *Washington Post*, June 6, 1986.

147–148 Yurchenko intelligence about Walker-Whitworth case: Martin affidavit submitted to U.S. District Court, San Francisco, August 1986, and Studeman affidavit to U.S. District Court, Baltimore, November 1986.

149–150 Martin attitudes toward plea bargaining with John and Michael Walker: Interviews with Dion, Carol Martin, Farmer, and Stephen Trott.

151 Lehman accomplishments as secretary of the navy: Trevor Armbrister, "Shaping Up the Navy," *Reader's Digest*, December 1985.

152 Meeting in Secretary Weinberger's office: Interview with Stephen Trott.

153 Schatzow statement: *Washington Post*, October 29, 1985.
Lehman denunciation of agreements with Walkers: *Washington Post*, October 30, 1985.
Weinberger rebuke of Lehman: *Washington Post*, November 2, 1985.

154 Dinner with Yurchenko: Multiple U.S. intelligence sources.

155 Yurchenko accusations: *Chicago Tribune*, November 8, 1985.

155–156 Thesis that Yurchenko was a controlled Soviet agent: a typical and comprehensive exposition of this thesis appears in *Life* magazine, September 1986. The author, Edward Jay Epstein, is an exponent of other conspiracy theories.

156–157 William Webster comments on Yurchenko case: "This Week with David Brinkley," December 1, 1985.

Chapter 9: Inside the Ring

page

158–160 Walker statements: Quoted statements were made in presence of author during interviews in San Diego, March 19 and 21 and April 3, 1986.

160ff. Walker's early life, initial years in navy and decision to approach Soviets: Navy interview, December 12, 1985; Transcript, pp. 24–2822–30; statements to author.

162–164 Walker's conversations inside Soviet embassy: FBI Interviews, October 30 and 31 and November 1, 4, 5, and 14, 1985.

164 Statement of Earl Clark: Transcript, pp. 11–1312–13.

165 Second Walker meeting with Soviets: FBI Interviews, October and November 1985; Transcript, pp. 24–2838–39, 24–2842.

166 Soviets' disinterest in submarines and subjects other than cryptographic data and operational and communications plans: Navy interview, December 12, 1985; FBI Interview, November 27, 1985; author's interviews.

167 Drop procedures followed by Walker: FBI Interview, November 14, 1985.

168–169 Walker espionage during 1968–69: Navy interview, December 12, 1985; Transcript, pp. 24–2845, 24–2861–62.

169–170 Walker assessment of Whitworth: FBI Interviews, October and November 1985.

170–173 Walker espionage aboard *Niagara Falls*: Navy interview, December 12, 1985; Transcript, p. 24–2871.

171 Walker forgery of background investigation report: Navy interview, December 12, 1985.

173–174 Recruitment of Whitworth: FBI Interview, November 27, 1985; Transcript, p. 24–2880.

175 Whitworth letter from Diego Garcia: Whitworth trial, Jury Book, p. 68.
Payment of eighteen thousand dollars to Whitworth: Graphic Chronology by Smits, entitled "Analysis of Whitworth Involvement with John Anthony Walker 1975–1985."

176 KGB reaction to Whitworth recruitment: FBI Interview, November 27, 1985; author's interviews.

177 Walker-Whitworth meeting in Hong Kong: FBI Interviews, November 14 and 27, 1985; Smits Graphic Chronology; author interviews with Walker.

177ff. Walker rendezvous with KGB in Casablanca: Ibid.

180–182 Instructions for Vienna rendezvous: Exhibit A-22-AA.

182–183 First Walker meeting with KGB in Vienna: FBI Interview, November 14, 1985; author's interviews.

184–197 passim All subsequent conversations between Walker and KGB officers in Vienna: Walker's accounts to Farmer, Dion, and Peterson and, during three interviews, to author.
All subsequent meetings between Walker and KGB, Walker and Whitworth: Previously cited FBI Interviews; Smits Graphic Chronology.

185–188 Espionage accomplishments of Whitworth aboard *Niagara Falls*: Transcript, p. 12–1443.

188 Whitworth pride in espionage: Walker account to Farmer.

190 Whitworth reaction to receipt of $100,000: Walker statement to Farmer and author.

190–191 Whitworth use of van: Interviews with Farmer and Schoggen.

194ff. Michael Walker's background, recruitment, and subsequent espionage: FBI Interviews, November 1, 13, 14, and 15, 1985.

197 Final Walker meeting with KGB in Vienna: Graphic Chronology; Walker statements to Farmer and author. The "Government's Sentencing Memorandum" submitted to the U.S. District Court for the District of Maryland in Baltimore in November 1986 states: "Analysts from the FBI and Navy have also compared Walker's recollection of the information compromised with that of his partner in espionage, Jerry Whitworth. Following his conviction in the Northern District of California, Jerry Whitworth agreed to speak with investigators. Like Walker, he has been debriefed and subjected to polygraph examinations over several weeks. The analysts have reviewed and compared the information provided by Whitworth with that provided by Walker. For the most part, Whitworth has corroborated John Walker's information concerning their espionage activities."

Chapter 10: Picking Up the Pieces

page

203 Lewin quotation: Lewin, *Ultra Goes to War*, 213–214.
Admiral Watkins's statement: *Washington Post,* June 12 and June 30, 1985.

203ff. Appointment and background of David Major: Interviews with Major, Smits, and Martin.

207 Tkachenko in Washington: State Department Diplomatic List, May 1985; Transcript, pp. 17–2060–2114; interview with Szady.
Reagan attitude toward Walker case: Interview with Major.

208–210 Studeman and Haver background: Interviews with Haver and Beverly Harrington, ONI; statement of Studeman to author.

210 Ability of Soviets to decipher enciphered U.S. communications without key material: Statements of Secretary of the Navy John Lehman, reported by *Washington Post,* October 30, 1985.

210–211 Deaths in Vietnam: Affidavit by Studeman to U.S. District Court, San Francisco, August 1986.

212 Lehman statements about potential consequences of case: *Washington Post,* October 30, 1985.
Studeman statements: Affidavit submitted to U.S. District Court, San Francisco, August 1986.

213 Carver background and statement: Transcript, pp. 45–5178–80, 45–5188, 45–5212; interview with Carver.

214ff. Expulsions of the Soviets were orally announced by State Department spokesmen. Intelligence sources confirmed the expulsions and revealed the positions of those expelled.

214 Required withdrawal of 105 Soviet "diplomats": U.S. Senate Select Committee on Intelligence Report, October 10, 1986, "Meeting the Espionage Challenge: A Review of U.S. Counterintelligence and Security Programs."
Belonogov statement: *Washington Post,* October 13, 1986.

215 U.S. expulsion of 25 Soviet intelligence officers: *New York Times,* October 28, 1986.

Soviet expulsion of 5 U.S. diplomats: Ibid.

217 Soviet withdrawal of employees in Moscow and Leningrad: *Washington Post,* October 23, 1986.

Index

Webster, William H., 149, 156
Weinberger, Caspar, 152, 153,
  207, 209
"Wentworth," see Whitworth,
  Jerry Alfred
Whitworth, Brenda Reis (Mrs.
  Jerry Alfred), 72, 76, 92, 123,
  133–134, 175, 185, 188, 190
Whitworth, Jerry Alfred: as
  "Wentworth," and search for,
  55, 57, 64, 69–76; in navy, 55,
  113–114, 122–129, 169–170,
  174–180, 183–194, (as CMS
  Custodian) 69, 75–76, 77,
  127–128, 175, 184, 188,
  (retires) 196, 198; located,
  identified as RUS, 74–78, 92,
  103–105, 114, 159 (see also
  RUS); as "D," 91, 92, 95,
  106, 112, 114, 197; FBI and,
  97, 101–105, 112, 222;

Walker's approach to, use of,
  see Walker, John Anthony,
  Jr.; case against, trial of, 114–
  115, 120–122, 129–137, 149–
  153, 158–160, 199–201, 206–
  207, 210–214, 218, 222; letter
  to Senator Byrd quoted, 126;
  KGB contact with, 184–194,
  196–197. See also Ciphers,
  U.S.
Wolfinger, Joseph T., 224; and
  Walker case, 45–47, 51, 53,
  58–59, 61, 79–87 passim, 95–
  96, 97, 107, 129, 132, 200, 206
World War II, 28–39, 166–167,
  202, 212, 218

Yorktown, USS, 31, 32
Yurchenko, Vitaly Sergeyevich,
  138–143, 144–148 passim,
  154–157, 203, 206, 210, 212,
  213, 221